D1238402

CANADA: NATION ON THE MARCH

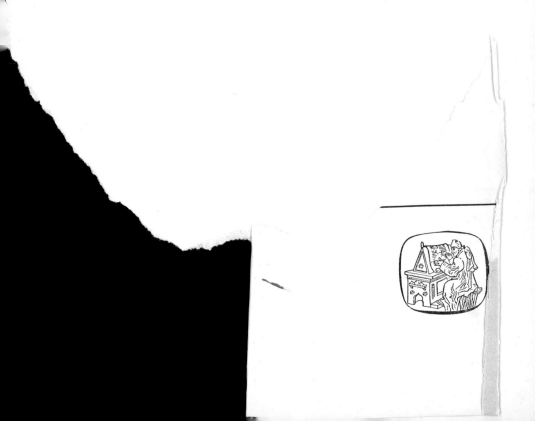

CANADA: NATION

LESTER B. PEARSON

W. A. MACKINTOSH

LOUIS RASMINSKY

HARVEY PERRY

PATRICK CONROY

ADELAIDE SINCLAIR

JOHN T. BRYDEN

ON THE MARCH

ROBERT H. WINTERS

RALPH P. BELL

JOHN G. DIEFENBAKER

JAMES S. DUNCAN

G. E. HALL

NATHAN E. TANNER

ROBERT M. FOWLER

E. J. UMPHREY

A. W. TRUEMAN

JEAN CHAUVIN

GRATTON O'LEARY

H. HUME WRONG

C. D. HOWE

CLARKE, IRWIN & COMPANY LIMITED

TORONTO, 1953

Printed in Canada
MARACLE PRESS LIMITED

ACKNOWLEDGMENTS

The portrait studies of Mr. Pearson, Mr. Bell, Mr. O'Leary and Mr. Wrong are by Karsh; those of Mr. Bryden and Mr. Tanner by Shelburne Studios, Inc., New York; of Mr. Winters and Mr. Howe by the National Film Board. Credit for the other portrait studies in this book is acknowledged as follows:

Dr. Mackintosh	*Fayer, New York*
Mr. Perry	*Thomas Studio*
Mr. Conroy	*T. V. Little, Ottawa*
Mr. Diefenbaker	*Paul Horsdal, Ottawa*
Mr. Duncan	*John Steele, Toronto*
Dr. Hall	*Leatherdale Studio, Toronto*
Mr. Fowler	*Dwight E. Dolan, Montreal*
Mr. Umphrey	*Milne*
Dr. Trueman	*Ibbotson*
Mr. Chauvin	*LaRose*

Top left   LESTER B. PEARSON

Top right   W. A. MACKINTOSH

Centre left   LOUIS RASMINSKY

Centre right   HARVEY PERRY

Bottom   PATRICK CONROY

Top left   ADELAIDE SINCLAIR

Top right   JOHN T. BRYDEN

Centre left   ROBERT H. WINTERS

Centre right   JOHN DIEFENBAKER

Bottom   RALPH P. BELL

Top left   E. J. UMPHREY

Top right   JAMES S. DUNCAN

Centre left   NATHAN E. TANNER

Centre right   ROBERT M. FOWLER

Bottom   G. E. HALL

Top left   A. W. Trueman

Top right   C. D. Howe

Centre left   H. Hume Wrong

Centre right   Gratton O'Leary

Bottom   Jean Chauvin

CONTENTS

ILLUSTRATIONS

INTRODUCTION

IN THE AUTUMN of 1952 Mr. Lyttleton B. P. Gould of New York approached the officers of The Town Hall Inc. with a suggestion that a lecture on Newfoundland as America's last frontier be included in plans for the forthcoming season. With Canada receiving an ever increasing press in the United States, due to its exciting postwar development, the directors felt that an entire series on Canada as a whole would be well received in New York. Accordingly, Dr. Thurston Davies sent his Assistant Director, Dr. John H. Powell, Jr., to Ottawa to explore such a possibility.

The Right Honourable C. D. Howe and the Honourable Dana Wilgress suggested to Dr. Powell that an ideal group to implement the idea would be the public relations men from Canadian industry and government who meet annually at the Seigniory Club to discuss Canadian information abroad. In the meantime a committee of distinguished financial, industrial and educational leaders in New York under the Chairmanship of Chancellor Heald of New York University and a Trustee of Town Hall had been formed to back the invitation to Canada and to promote the series. Dr. Powell met with a warm response when he told the story to the group meeting at the Seigniory Club. Mr. Herbert Richardson, chairman of the meeting, appointed a working committee of Canadians consisting of Don Henshaw as chairman, I. S. Decarie, Bruce Keith, Ivan Lenard, John Martin and Frank Prendergast. This committee began immediate sessions with the New York working committee of which Mr. Gould was chairman, with B. H. Holdsworth, William Honneus, Taylor Mills and Dr. Powell as members.

A programme under the title of "Canada: Nation on the March" was drafted, lists of speakers from the several fields of Canadian activity were nominated and tentative dates set for the series.

In the meantime Mr. H. L. Enman, President of The Bank of Nova Scotia, accepted the invitation of the Canadian working committee to form a sponsoring committee. From every province and every phase of Canadian life came a quick response and a most representative group of men took their places on the committee. The invitations to the people nominated as speakers to represent Canada met with a hearty response.

The series began on March 3rd, 1953, and concluded on April 7th. The contents of this book are a record of what was said at Town Hall during those memorable Tuesday afternoons. No record, however, can be compiled of the friendly atmosphere in which the lectures were given, the eager interest shown by the audiences, the intelligent and searching questions asked at the receptions and dinners which followed each session, or, above all, the warmth with which New York welcomed their neighbours from Canada.

We of the Sponsoring Committees are most grateful to all who made the Canadian series an important contribution to international understanding: the officials of Town Hall, the two working committees, and to our speakers who so truly represented Canada.

HENRY T. HEALD
Chairman,
New York Sponsoring
Committee

H. L. ENMAN
Chairman,
Canadian Sponsoring
Committee

22 May, 1953

THE INTERNATIONAL SITUATION

THE RIGHT HONOURABLE LESTER B. PEARSON is at present the Secretary of State for External Affairs of Canada. For several years he was attached to the Canadian Embassy in Washington, holding the rank of Canadian Ambassador to the United States from 1944 to 1946. He is now President of the General Assembly of the United Nations.

I

THE INTERNATIONAL SITUATION

THE CHAPTER with which I am to initiate these discussions on Canada is entitled "Canada's International Situation and Point of View". The "personal columns" in our newspapers often speak of "situations wanted". Sometimes in international affairs we find ourselves in situations which no one in his right mind could possibly want. The international situation in which Canadians find themselves, like that facing other people, is only *partly* the product of what we are and what we want. Much of it is ready made for us by the hard and sometimes bitter facts of international life.

Canada is a North American nation in a British Commonwealth, made up of peoples as old—and as new—as any on this continent, with a varied and expanding economy and with inherited traditions of political liberty and respect for law. All these elements are reflected in Canadian attitudes towards other peoples, and in the policies we advocate and support in our relations with them.

There is something else, however: an awareness of the importance to us of the policies of other states. Our whole history tells us that events far from Canadian borders can transform overnight our lives and our destinies; can re-shape the whole pattern of our economy, our daily ways of life and work. We know from hard experience that we cannot dodge the impact of world events. Sentiment, derived from an unbroken political association with the United Kingdom, and a continued contact with France, reinforces and underlines this knowledge.

Canadians cannot avoid playing some part in world affairs, for this is dictated by our history and tradition, by our national interests, as well as by the kind of world we live in.

Our first interest is in peace. To seek and secure this is the primary obligation of any government of Canada. This is natural for we have—apart from the Korean conflict—been at war for ten years since 1914.

The realization of this desire for peace and security, we know, depends on a recognition of its vital and equal importance by others. We accept the reality of inter-dependence in a shrinking world. Peace for us means that there must be peace in the international community.

A second national concern — closely tied also to international developments—is the welfare and the prosperity of our people, which is inseparable from the welfare and prosperity of others.

Canada is a country which to an unparalleled extent is dependent on world trade for the livelihood of its people. Our trade links with the United States, the United Kingdom and the Commonwealth, with Western Europe and with the rest of the world, both for necessary imports and as markets for our exports, give us a vital stake in a high and increasing level of world trade, second to no other country in the world, and a great stake in world prosperity which, like peace, is also indivisible.

What then are these fundamental principles which so largely determine the conduct of foreign policy in Canada, irrespective of what government or party may happen to be in power?

First, there is *national unity*. No policy can be regarded as wise which divides the people whose effort and resources must put it into effect. In Canada this applies not only to the two main cultural groups; it applies equally to sectionalism of any kind. For Canada disunity means impotence. The possibility of such disunity is always an immediate and intense pre-occupation with any Canadian Government conscious of the facts of our geography, of our history and of our racial and federal structure.

Then, there is secondly *political liberty*. We value political freedom as something beyond price. So we are conscious of the danger to our own political institutions when freedom is attacked in other parts of the world. From our democratic inheritance, and from our own experience, we have come as a people to dislike and distrust governments which rule by force and suppress freedom. We seek — and find — our friends among those of like political traditions. And we recognize that a threat to the liberty of peoples elsewhere is a threat to our liberties at home.

Thirdly, there is *the rule of law in national and international affairs*. Respect for the rule of law, both in our own country, and in the relations we wish to see established between the states of

4

CANADA AT THE UNITED NATIONS

We do not seek merely "peace in our time", but in the time of generations whose future is now in our hands. Above all, it must be peace on terms which free men can respect.

THE NRX REACTOR AT CHALK RIVER, ONTARIO

Canada, the great producer of uranium, since the war has been expending its research energies towards the utilization of atomic energy, fission products, and radio-active isotopes, for a peace-time economy.

the international community, is for us a cardinal principle. This is one of the elements in our national attitude towards totalitarian countries, whether of left or right, where the government sets itself above the law. It also helps to explain the support we give to strengthening the procedures of law and justice in the international community.

And there is, as a source of our conduct, the recognition of *the importance of moral values.* In our national life and in our participation in world affairs, we are deeply conscious of the moral values which we have inherited from older civilizations. This is the basis of the importance which we give to the individual personality in the conduct of human relations.

The final principle is the *acceptance of responsibility in keeping with our conception of our role in world affairs.* Our experience has shown us that our security depends upon the development of a successfully functioning international organization. We are, therefore, prepared to play our full part in associations and organizations which serve the world community, within our capacities and our resources and our wealth.

These are the principles, very broadly and very generally stated, which influence and largely determine our point of view on world affairs. Our experience in two world wars—and their aftermath—has confirmed our belief in the validity of these principles.

In August 1914 Canada was a young country on the eve of great developments, with a population only about half of what it is today. After four years of what was called the First Great War, sixty thousand of our youth were left on the battlefields of France and of Flanders. That experience remains with us an abiding memory, but at first we did not draw the correct conclusions from it, and we were not alone in the world in that respect.

After the first war, many of us pinned our hopes for peace on the newly-founded League of Nations, without showing any great zeal in taking measures necessary to realize these hopes. Governments — certainly including the Canadian Government — were not prepared to use collective force to deter aggression at the point when and where it might have been stopped. So, by September 1939 there was no way to stop Hitler's Germany short of a total

5

war based on old concepts of national defence and improvised national alliances.

In the six years of total war which followed—in that war for which we did not find a name, merely a number—forty-two thousand Canadians lost their lives. The monetary cost to Canada's twelve million people was in the neighbourhood of twenty billion dollars.

But in these second war and post-war years, all of us learned some lessons of great importance about peace. We were given a second chance and we showed signs at least of taking advantage of it. We learned that peace could not be achieved by leaving the job of securing it to others; by refusing to make commitments in advance; or by shutting our eyes to the reality of the threat of force designed to achieve world domination. Above all, we learned that in the face of a determined aggressor, to be weak was to invite disaster, and to be alone was to ensure defeat.

In 1945, from the rubble and destruction of World War II, there emerged a great hope and a great principle. The hope was that through the United Nations we might succeed, in the words of the Charter, "in saving succeeding generations from the scourge of war which twice in our lifetime has brought untold sorrow to mankind."

Canada's support for the United Nations at that time, and her support now, is based on the principle that aggression could only be prevented or defeated through the organization of collective security. That principle was right in 1945, and it is right today. But we — and others — were gradually forced, through our experience of the events of 1945, '46 and '47, to recognize that the unanimity of the Great Powers on which the prospect of collective security through United Nations action was originally planned had yielded to mistrust and then to deep hostility. Instead of the peace for which we so earnestly hoped, we felt the icy breath of the "cold war."

So we were compelled by events to organize the collective security envisaged under the Charter through other more limited agencies, such as the North Atlantic Treaty Organization. In company with other free states in the Atlantic community and elsewhere, and in response to the threat we felt, and the fear we felt, Canada decided to increase and to pool its defence effort, and to assume, in advance, far-reaching and precise commitments for collective defence and security.

To show how far in our country we have advanced in that respect, it is only necessary to contemplate what would have been the atmosphere, what would have been the reaction in the House of Commons in Ottawa in 1935, say, if any Prime Minister or any representative of the government had risen in the House and asked the House to accept the proposition that an attack on Turkey was automatically an attack on Canada; but that proposition has recently been made and accepted without a dissenting voice in our Parliament.

Then in June 1950, the agression in Korea exposed the global nature of the threat to us all. When it broke on an almost unsuspecting world, the United Nations reacted with a speed and vigour which heartened its friends and confounded its critics, thanks, of course, to certain circumstances which were accidental at the time in the Security Council and may not be easily repeated. The Korean aggression placed a large sector of the free world on the alert. It showed the immensity of the challenge. It exposed the nature of the forces—both physical and psychological—which the free world faced, and the vast dimensions of the struggle in which our generation was engaged.

Forces from Canada, and other members of the United Nations moved to the scene of battle alongside their comrades from the United States, who, with the free Koreans, bore, and continue to bear, the brunt of the struggle there.

These events across the Pacific had an immediate effect on NATO planning in Europe. Effective forces and equipment were stationed in increasing numbers on the frontiers where history and experience have convinced us the main immediate danger still lies.

They are there for one reason only—to deter or to resist aggression and to make peace possible. Canadians, almost without exception, approve of our own participation in this effort.

The price Canadians are paying for the maintenance of our growing defences, at home and abroad, is, for a nation of less than fifteen millions, substantial. In 1939 we were spending only about thirty-eight million dollars for defence in Canada. This year we are spending more than two billion dollars, or, in terms of the total national income of the United States, the equivalent of about thirty-eight billion dollars. And since World War II, we have given assistance to our friends and in doing so to ourselves in the form of grants, gifts, or credits to the equivalent in terms of United States' national income of nearly forty billions of dollars.

Both in Europe and in Korea, Canada is bearing its own substantial share of the common burden. The Canadian contribution may be small measured in absolute terms compared with the gigantic effort of the United States. But no country in the world of our size and position is doing more in practical terms to fulfil its international obligations and responsibilities, and we are doing it at a time when the development of new resources in Canada presents us with a great challenge and takes up much of our energy and our strength.

We feel this effort is necessary because at this point in the middle of the twentieth century, Mr. Churchill's "terrible twentieth century", Canada sees, across the Atlantic and the Pacific, an international picture full of tension and danger, coming to sharp focus in Asia where actual fighting is now going on.

In carrying out her policies, the three most important of the associations to which Canada belongs are the Commonwealth, NATO, the United Nations. Each of these has its distinctive contribution to make to the outcome of our search for security.

A word first about the Commonwealth.

This uncommon, indeed unique, association of free and independent states emerging from the old dependent Empire is rooted deep in our history in Canada. In the contemporary world, it has an importance and a value which no one should underestimate in adding up the resources of the free world.

Unlike the United Nations, unlike NATO, the Commonwealth has no formal machinery, no treaty binding its members, no specific commitments. In its very freedom and in its diversity lies its power and influence, which it can wield for good in the world today.

The modern Commonwealth is no narrow group aiming to improve its position at the expense of others. It is a widely representative association, aware of the great range of conditions throughout most of the world, seeking to find some basis on which national actions can be taken in the light of the needs of international co-operation; and, above all at this time, linking together Asia and the West when links of this kind are so sorely needed.

Then there is NATO. Canada looks to NATO as the shield of its own defence in Europe and the Atlantic area, and as the nucleus of a community of peace-loving Atlantic states co-operating for the common good. NATO threatens no one, for none of its members has aggressive intentions. Its purpose is to reduce fear and tension in the face of threats and provocation. Whatever has been achieved to this end in Europe since 1949, is due to the determination of the members of the NATO coalition to build and to maintain a powerful deterrent force against aggression in free Europe.

That deterrent force is being built and will be maintained so long as it is necessary. As our contribution to it, since the autumn of 1951, the 27th Canadian Infantry Brigade has been stationed in Western Europe. Twenty-four ships of the Canadian Navy have been made available to the Supreme Commander, Atlantic. These will be increased until by 1954 they will number fifty-two. Twelve jet fighter squadrons of the Royal Canadian Air Force, an Air Division, part of which is already overseas, will be stationed in Europe by next year.

We are also making a substantial contribution to NATO in the form of mutual aid to our allies and partners. Increasing amounts have been made available in each budget since September 1950, and the appropriation for the current financial year amounts to about 325 million dollars. These appropriations provide for transfers of equipment, the training of air crew of our other NATO partners, and other material aid where it is needed.

NATO, however, is or should be more than a military alliance against aggression. While it came into being because it was found that the United Nations was powerless, in the circumstances that existed, to provide the security we sought, it rests on foundations more durable than military strength alone. The force which unites the communities of the North Atlantic area is not only a common danger; it is also a common history and a common tradition of freedom. To achieve our aims, economic and political stability and co-operation must co-exist with military strength, for military strength bought at the expense of economic or political stability is illusory.

Thus, from the outset, Canadian policy has aimed at ensuring that NATO should promote co-operation and progress in areas out-side the purely military sphere. Progress in these areas has been disappointingly slow. We hope, however, that it is sure. We realize that it must come from within, and cannot, with success, be forced into any pre-conceived pattern. Progress will depend upon the growth of mutual confidence and understanding, rather than on procedures or committees. But non-military progress in this field there must be if NATO is to survive the emergency which gave it birth.

The third club we belong to is the United Nations. In Canada, we have not forgotten that we share with fifty-nine other countries common membership in our world organization, the United Nations. We continue to support the aims and purposes inscribed in its Charter.

The principles of general collective security, and general collective welfare, remain the basis of our foreign policy. We are convinced—Korea is the proof—that aggression in any part of the world constitutes, in the long run, a threat to every other part. Our acceptance of this principle, or at any rate its application in practice, is qualified, as are so many things in this world, by the available resources at our disposal. To say we must use judgment in deciding how the collective security obligations of the Charter can best be discharged means merely an acceptance of reality.

But while we must recognize that collective action to meet aggression may have to vary according to circumstances, the collective response to aggression in Korea, and the adoption of the Uniting for Peace resolution of November 1950, are evidences of the growing determination of the majority of members of the United Nations to work towards the achievement of the kind of collective security envisaged in the United Nations Charter. As an evidence of our faith, nearly twenty thousand Canadians have seen service, on land, on sea, and in the air, in the Korean theatre of operations.

Above all the United Nations is a world forum which gives its members—on both sides of the Great Divide—an organized means of negotiation and conciliation when the time and the nations are ripe for it, and when there are tangible indications that the will to seek peaceful solutions exists.

The United Nations resolution on Korea united fifty-four nations of every continent, and illustrated in dramatic fashion the unique role which our world organization can play in bridging differences between countries sharing a common purpose.

It will be seen that in the world situation in which Canadians find themselves, this peace we seek, is compounded, like all things that are durable, of diverse elements. For us, peace is not an uneasy pause between bouts of localized aggression, nor a slow retreat in the face of brute force. If that is what the Communist world means by "co-existence", there would be little point, for us, in "co-existing." We do not seek merely "peace in our time", but in the time of generations whose future is now in our hands. Above all, it must be peace on terms which free men can respect.

The United Nations—NATO—the British Commonwealth; in each, Canada participates and expresses its point of view frankly and fully and in recognizably Canadian accents; each moulds and influences Canada's foreign policy. In the minds of Canadians there is no conflict in our obligations to these organizations and associations since they seek a common purpose. This common purpose is the achievement of a progressive and peaceful world community in which freedom reigns. We are under no illusion that the achievement of this purpose will be anything but a slow and laborious process. We know that we shall at times find it difficult to keep our distant goal in sight.

Today, Canada looks out on the world with anxiety, but also with confidence—a confidence based on the progress made by the free nations so far in the search for peace through international co-operation; on the strength and on the fundamental wisdom of the nations with which our destiny is so closely linked; and on the faith that in collective action under the leadership of a powerful and peaceful United States of America lies the best hope for the future of the world community of which we are a part.

THE PEOPLE AND THEIR HISTORY

Dr. W. A. Mackintosh is now Principal of Queen's University, Kingston, Ontario. He is a graduate of Queen's University and was previously a member of the Department of Political and Economic Science and Dean of the Faculty of Arts. In 1951 he was appointed Principal and became the first Queen's graduate to hold this office.

II

THE PEOPLE AND THEIR HISTORY

IN TERMS of its population Canada is a small country. In area
Canada is larger than the United States, but it is not nearly so
large as it is portrayed on a Mercator projection map, which somewhat exaggerates its importance. There is, also, in its area a very
generous space provided for permanently built-in refrigerating
equipment in the northern latitudes. Canada's history goes back
three and a half centuries, despite the fact that it seems to be considered a new, or recently, or almost arrived nation. Now numbers,
space and time are all formidable dimensions to encompass in a
brief chapter, and if a fourth dimension is added, namely the
essential characteristics of this northern people, it all becomes very
difficult indeed.

Canadians, I think, are generally rather pleased, at the moment,
and a trifle confused, to find that they themselves and their country
are attracting a good deal of attention to which in their modest way
they have not been accustomed. The world press is spotted with
feature articles extolling Canada as a land of opportunity and freedom, a country with great possibilities for the future and even a few
assets in its heritage from the past. The federal budget and the
changes that are made there in taxes, which a decade ago would
have got barely a couple of lines of type in the press of other
countries, are now given extended space in both the news and the
editorial pages of the metropolitan press of the world. That the
most highly valued dollar in the world is the Canadian dollar draws
some further attention and is noted even in great money markets
like New York. All through the western world there is a good deal
of talk about newly discovered resources in Canada, oil, iron,
copper, nickel, titanium, uranium, and a lot of still rarer metals.
People talk about petro-chemistry and wood chemistry and their
relation to our industry. They talk about all the industries that go
with water power, but they have learned also that Canadians produce

not only newsprint for the presses, but also jet engines for the defence of the western world. They see a very impressive inflow of capital from the United States into Canada. The people abroad need to be reminded, perhaps, that this inflow, impressive as it is, is only about 14 per cent of the capital which is currently being invested in Canada, and that Canadians themselves are supplying the other 86 per cent. On the other hand it is well to remind Canadians that the inflow of capital from the United States is not entirely drawn by the attractiveness of Canada. It is to some extent impelled by the relative unattractiveness of other areas of investment. Canadians are perhaps even more impressed to find themselves praised as a people of good judgment, sober industry, and even of political stability. It is possible that they could be induced to be a little complacent about this.

The purpose of this chapter is to sketch in rather brief compass some background, to provide some framework so that what is happening in Canada today, as it will be described in other chapters in this book, may be seen with some perspective and reduced to some kind of scale.

The people of Canada, in origin, are very similar to the people of the United States. Both countries began as colonies of European civilizations. Both have been shaped by the environment in which they have lived, by the changes in the world outside, and by the challenges which they have met in the course of their experience. True, Canada had not as many Cambridge graduates among its first settlers as are claimed by the people of New England and very few of its first ancestors remembered the name of the ship on which they came over. These, however, are quite minor differences; but there are two differences that are more decisive.

The first and most obvious one is that about 30 per cent of Canadians are French speaking. Though their ancestors originated in France, they are not now nor for generations have they been French. They are Canadians who speak French. With minor exceptions, the rest of the population speaks English of varying sorts. In the course of their history these two groups have confronted each other with serious and difficult problems of political unity and the basis of community living. These have, on the whole, been surmounted because increasingly, despite differences in language, to some extent in religion, to a large extent in inherited background, each group is Canadian. This fact in Canada's history has led to some important consequences, some important Canadian characteristics. Every Canadian politician, if he has survived, has learned lessons in moderation. Each political group has learned that there are questions in Canadian politics which must be compromised, that there are areas in which logic and preconceptions cannot be pushed to the limit. It would be an extremely ignorant Canadian politician indeed who was not acutely aware that national unity and indeed national survival have depended through Canada's history on toleration. Canadians have now gone far beyond this point. They have gone to the point where there is recognition by each group of the particular virtues which the other language group brings into the national life.

This is the first and perhaps the greatest difference as between the people of the United States and those of Canada. But there is a second difference, perhaps less important, certainly less obvious. To no significant degree has the course of Canadian history required Canadians to turn their backs on Europe or endeavour to isolate themselves from it. Through no particular merit of their own, the establishment of Canadian autonomy was achieved without any violent rupture, and without the setting up of inhibitions and resentments, at least no greater than those which might be considered normal between older and younger people. The existence of two language groups, the continuity of Canada's relations with the Commonwealth of Nations, these are two facts which might well be remembered when trying to assess Canadian qualities and assets.

In the world outside Canadians have the reputation for being cautious, or even over-cautious. They may even be considered a little slow. In fact, however, the historical evidence is overwhelming that in terms of their environment the opposite has been true. The extension of boundaries, the building of railways, the setting up of the machinery of government, the machinery for the administration of justice, have always tended in Canada's history to outrun the limits of settlement. In the course of United States' history there were periods when it was difficult for the apparatus of transportation and government to catch up with the rapidity of settlement. In contrast, Canada went through long periods of waiting for the possibilities of settlement to catch up with the projects which had been set out for government and for economic expansion. The bases of economic development in the northern half of the continent have disclosed themselves slowly and reluctantly. Opportunity waited on technical development and on world markets. Plans and organizations have frequently been far ahead of opportunity.

There is, originating in the United States primarily, a variety of escapist literature whose very slender roots of reality go back to the days of a wild and lawless West. There is no genuine Canadian counterpart. Into the Canadian substitute for this literary genre ride the Royal Canadian Mounted Police. They were there before the cattle rustler, which makes it an entirely different kind of story. Now the Mountie is a well known Canadian symbol. He symbolizes quite an important fact in Canadian history. He has waited there for decades in his red coat and it is only in the last few years that technical practice has caught up with him and tourists have arrived with colour films and been able to take his picture in his full glory. Canadians, like the Mountie, have waited long decades for technical developments and other changes to catch up and to bring the full riches of their resources into the picture. Sometimes they even have to wait for their neighbours. They have become used to waiting for their neighbours to make up their minds about the St. Lawrence Deep Waterway, but when it comes to waiting for them to make up their minds as to whether or not they *have* made up their minds, then Canadian patience is tried.

The long struggle to uncover the resources of the northern half of this continent has, with other factors, had another effect upon Canadians which is perhaps worth noting. The average Canadian has something less than enthusiasm for arguing the merit of private versus public enterprise. One of the greatest public enterprises in Canada, the Hydro-Electric Power Commission of Ontario, was created by a government which was as conservative as Calvin Coolidge. There is no record of any Canadian pioneer community which refused a railway unless it was privately owned. They preferred it privately owned, but that was not the point. They wanted a railway. They believed in what would get them a railway, for at times in Canadian history railways were hard to come by. If there is little prejudice about public ownership, there is no enthusiasm for it. It is a sufficiently familiar phenomenon in Canada that the average Canadian is skeptical of enthusiastic claims, but if in Canada a more dispassionate view on this matter is found than in the United States on the one hand or in Europe on the other hand, it has simply grown out of the hard facts of our history.

The union into which several parts of Canada entered about eighty-six years ago was not, as in the United States, a union of thirteen compact Atlantic colonies, nor was it concerned with freedom from an empire. It was a much more humdrum affair than that. It was the union of four widely separated, small, even tiny, areas of population. In the east was a maritime settlement, thrust far out into the north Atlantic, so far that Montreal, which is nearly 1,000 miles inland, is nearer to Liverpool than is New York. Beyond the Appalachian Highlands lay the St. Lawrence River and the Great Lakes, which form a gateway into the interior of the continent which to a notable degree has its resources lying in the interior. The St. Lawrence valley is divided between those Canadians who speak English and those Canadians who speak French. Away across the pre-Cambrian Shield there was a tiny settlement in the heart of the continent in the Red River Valley, and nearly 2,000 miles farther on across a vacant prairie and over the Rocky Mountains were the little settlements on the British Columbia coast. The bringing together of these isolated islands involved a great project to link them by railway transportation, to provide the St. Lawrence and the Great Lakes with a hinterland and, very important, to see that the hinterland was attached to the Great Lakes from the north and not from the south at Chicago. It was a project also to make the interchange of trade between these regions a basis for Canadian industry.

It was an almost fantastically optimistic project, but it was carried through. The West was taken over from the Hudson's Bay Company. By an enormous effort and acceptance of great risks, the Canadian Pacific Railway was built; the whole structure of a vast project was set up; and then for a decade nothing happened. For a time it looked as if the Canadian Pacific Railway would never achieve its proud record of being just about the only railway on this continent which has not gone through a receivership. Then in the middle of the 'nineties there was a change, and out to Europe and the United Kingdom from the prairies flowed Canadian wheat; and into the prairies flowed British Columbian lumber and the manufactures of Ontario and Quebec, and heavy industry grew up to make rails and track fastenings for the railways. Capital flowed in then, mostly from London, and from Europe and the United States there came immigrants in the largest numbers that Canada had ever experienced. This was the period in which Canada came nearest to matching the great experience of the United States with its westward moving frontier of the nineteenth century. But it never did match the United States' experience. The challenges that confronted Canada were different challenges and Canadians made different responses. The Canadian frontier soon became a northern frontier, a perpetual frontier driven back periodically in deep thrusts as new devices made it possible to conquer and use new resources.

The second period of Canadian expansion, after 1920, brought into play not the resources of farm lands, but those of the pre-Cambrian Shield, that great area of granite, rock, muskeg and clay belts in the depressed centre of which lies Hudson Bay. The great rise of the metropolitan press in the United States, with its insatiable demand for newsprint, tossed out in extras in World War I and in fantastic Sunday supplements ever since — this rise of the United States press brought the spruce, the water storage which the beaver helped to create and the water power which no one else wanted to use together into a great paper industry. By 1925 new techniques had been developed for using well known resources of highly complex ores and gave rise to a greatly enlarged non-ferrous metal industry. The power that was developed for paper was extended to electro-metallurgy. With a larger population and higher incomes, the automotive industry came in, to change the direction of steel producing away from the old rail methods. This was the second era, but of course it ended in the almost bottomless pit of the 'thirties.

What is happening now in Canada is a third great era of expansion, greater in some ways than those which had gone before, and, on the whole, more peculiarly Canadian. The search for oil, which men knew was there, is finally being rewarded in great abundance. The revolution in the use of light metals has sent companies still further north in their search for unused power resources. There has been a revolution in the technique of discovering metallic

GOLD MINING AT YELLOWKNIFE, NORTHWEST TERRITORIES

In the northland, the great areas of the Northwest Territories and the Yukon, there are still vast frontiers of natural resources which have not yet been fully explored and scarcely touched.

LANDING BARGES AT URANIUM BEAVERLODGE
SASKATCHEWAN

The bases of economic development in the northern half of the continent have disclosed themselves slowly and reluctantly. Opportunity waited on technical development and on world markets.

resources. In Canada there used to be an old and tried method of mineral discovery. Someone built a railway, usually a costly railway, preferably a transcontinental railway, and it was hoped that in the unavoidable rock cuts necessary in its construction valuable mineral resources would be discovered. It rather reminds one of Charles Lamb's account of how the Chinese produced roast pig, but it had this important difference, that it required Canada to build something rather than to burn it down. Now even to slow thinking Canadians it became obvious that the whole northern half of the continent could not be explored by this expensive method. But any method which could discover the Sudbury nickel copper area, and the Cobalt silver area, and half a dozen other mineral areas in Canada is not to be scoffed at. What has taken place recently is that with magnetometers and gravimeters and geiger counters and other contraptions mineral metallic resources may be discovered even though they lie under great over-burdens of rock and soil and when these are combined with the aeroplane, better explosives, and modern earth-moving equipment, it is easy to see that the great, stubborn, reluctant northern frontier is on the move.

But there is another side, the need for resources. The war and its aftermath have brought about a vast speeding up of industrialization and urbanization in the United States and elsewhere. The industrial intake of materials has enormously increased. In all of the underdeveloped territories of the world there is pressure towards industrialization, some of it a mistaken pressure, and those countries which have metals, and wood, and oil, and power, and other materials for sale are in a favourable position. Something else has happened, which is of importance. In addition to these great developments in exploiting the mine and forest, Canada is still an important producer of food, and there has been a revolution in the world of food. There has been a great diversion of sources. Manchuria as a source of Japanese food has disappeared behind the Iron Curtain. Eastern Europe as a source of food for western Europe has similarly been withdrawn. Revolution and civil disturbance have disastrously reduced the output of the great rice bowl of South East Asia. A larger portion of the western world, both European and Asiatic, has had to turn to North America for food. Canada is in the food business.

These are circumstances which, together with all the factors which affect the whole western world, create the present position of the Canadian economy and the prosperity of the Canadian people. It is striking that in these rapid changes, Canada's economy has not become more self-sufficient than it was, except in the cases of oil and iron ore. Canada has followed the same direction as before, the continued development of great specialized exports, of unprocessed and partly processed materials and food. Of course, with more production, more people, more consumer spending, the economy has also gained in depth and in the variety of its industries. Now, these changes have been speeded up by rearmament and the Korean War, but they have not been created by these forces. They constitute a general and permanent change in the level and scope of Canadian economic activity.

What is taking place has reinforced and extended the close relationship between Canada and the United States. The degree of dependence on the United States as a market for Canada's exports has increased and there is perhaps some danger that the recession in the United States, which is always being advertised in advance, might create a serious, though temporary, contraction in Canadian activity. But in other ways the changes that are taking place will strengthen rather than weaken the essentially Canadian characteristics of the country. The hard facts of geology and climate determine that Canadians could never really imitate in their history the great western expansion of the United States. There have been only intermittent instalments of that. Canada's is a different kind of frontier, which calls not for great numbers of farm settlers, but for the tools of modern science and the apparatus of great industry. It is a frontier which will never disappear, will never wholly be conquered. Successful inroads will be made on it and to the challenges which it offers the Canadian people will make their response; and in that process Canadian characteristics will be reinforced and created.

The relationship of Canada to the United States has been and will continue to be close. The two countries have many similarities, for in part they share a common experience in the development of North America. Always the largest metropolitan centres of the continent will lie in the United States and the pull of the metropolis does not stop at international boundaries; but Canada has other relations, to the Commonwealth of Nations, to the North Atlantic Treaty. NATO will always appear to a Canadian as perhaps somewhat less of an emergency organization and somewhat more of a natural grouping than it does to the people of the United States, for from the time when the first fishermen came to the banks of Newfoundland and remained to establish what are parts of Canada today, Canadians have felt in their bones the strategic significance, a significance in world development, of the narrowness of the north Atlantic.

Canada's form of government is a parliamentary government which is derived from Britain. Canadians believe that it is a form which leads to better and clearer political decisions, but they go no further than to say it is a better form of government for them. In origin it is a British form of government, but Canadians of British extraction are no more apt in its strategy and tactics than are Canadians whose ancestors long ago came from France. In any list of notable Canadian parliamentarians French speaking Canadians would appear in rather greater proportion than their relative numbers in the population would justify.

If its beginning is dated from the earliest settlements in Nova Scotia and Quebec, Canada's history goes back as far or further than that of the United States, and if one is to understand Canada today, one must understand something of the reasons for this delayed development, something of the stubborn challenges of an environment, something of the stage in world history in which Canada's resources have come to be needed. These not only explain the history of Canada, they explain something of the characteristics of the people; but one needs to know something also of the origins of the Canadian people and of the influences which have made them Canadian.

Geologically young soils show the characteristics of the parent geological material from which they come, but eventually, by the passage of time, all the soils of a region assume characteristics which are determined for them by the climate and the vegetation of the region in which they are. Now the diverse components which make up the people of Canada are being modified by an analogous process and there has emerged from the facts and challenges of history a

Canadian who had his origin in Europe, who is British in his political affiliations, who is and always will be greatly influenced by his neighbours in the United States, but who, most of all, is just himself.

THE CANADIAN DOLLAR

MR. LOUIS RASMINSKY is Executive Assistant to the Governors of the Bank of Canada. For many years he was Chairman Alternate of the Canadian Foreign Exchange Control Board. At the Financial and Monetary Conference held at Bretton Woods in 1944, he acted as Chairman of the Drafting Committee on the International Monetary Fund. He is at present an executive director of the Fund and of the International Bank for Reconstruction and Development.

III

THE CANADIAN DOLLAR

FEW RECENT EVENTS have done more to focus American attention on Canada than the rise in the foreign exchange value of the Canadian dollar during the past year or so. Before October, 1950, when the Canadian Government decided to unpeg the Canadian currency and allow its value to be determined in the free market, you could buy a Canadian dollar in the United States for ninety cents in American money. That was the official price of the Canadian dollar, our official exchange rate. The freeing of the Canadian dollar was followed by a steady rise in its value on the foreign exchange markets of the world. Today in the United States you have to pay about $1.02 American to get a Canadian dollar.

I am going to try to explain what significance should be attached to the rise in the foreign exchange value of the Canadian dollar since the freeing of the exchange rate in October 1950. But before doing that, I would like to say something about what significance should *not* be attached to it. First of all I would like to dispose of the fallacy that the current rate of exchange reflects in some literal but mysterious way the relative economic strengths of Canada and the United States. The fact that the Canadian dollar is now quoted at about $1.02 in American money leads people to speak of it as being at a premium of 2 per cent over the American dollar. This is convenient and probably inevitable. But the Canadian dollar is a separate and distinct currency unit from the American dollar. It would be a mistake to think, because the Canadian and the American currency units both happen to be called by the same name — dollars — that there is some necessary relationship between them, whether at par or at some other rate, which should be regarded as normal.

The significant thing about the Canadian dollar is that it has risen substantially in price in the last couple of years, and not that it is quoted at a premium over the American dollar. The fact that the Canadian dollar is currently quoted in the exchange markets at $1.02 American does not mean that Canadians are 2 per cent more intelligent or 2 per cent more virtuous and certainly not 2 per cent richer than Americans.

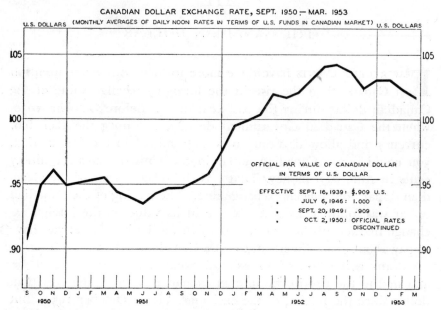

CANADIAN DOLLAR EXCHANGE RATE, SEPT. 1950 — MAR. 1953

(MONTHLY AVERAGES OF DAILY NOON RATES IN TERMS OF U.S. FUNDS IN CANADIAN MARKET)

OFFICIAL PAR VALUE OF CANADIAN DOLLAR
IN TERMS OF U.S. DOLLAR

EFFECTIVE SEPT. 16, 1939 : $.909 U.S.
" JULY 6, 1946 : 1.000 "
" SEPT. 20, 1949 : .909 "
" OCT. 2, 1950 : OFFICIAL RATES
DISCONTINUED

Now why has the Canadian dollar become a more expensive commodity in the past year or two? In a free exchange market, such as we have in Canada, the foreign currency price of the Canadian dollar is determined by supply and demand, just like any other price. If the foreign demand for Canadian dollars increases relative to our demand for foreign currencies, the Canadian dollar exchange rate is bid up to a higher level. This is exactly what has happened during the past year or so. Foreign demand for Canadian dollars increased sharply because people in other countries wanted to step up their buying of goods and services from us, and because they wanted to invest more money in the development of Canada and in Canadian long-term security offerings. On the other side of the market, i.e., the demand side in Canada, Canadian demand for foreign currencies, whether to pay for goods and services or make investments abroad, rose only slightly. The result was a bidding up of the exchange rate to a point where additional supplies of Canadian dollars were tempted on to the exchange market.

You will appreciate that this little sketch of how the Canadian exchange market works is drastically oversimplified. So far as it goes, it is reasonably accurate—but it does not go very far. Why have foreigners recently bought more and invested more in Canada, and why has Canadian demand for foreign goods, services and investments lagged behind? In order to answer these questions, it is necessary to examine some of the changes which have been taking place recently in the Canadian economy.

The rise in the Canadian dollar has occurred at a time when the Canadian economy is expanding very rapidly. Contributors of other chapters to this book are going to describe in detail the recent development of our productive resources and I do not intend to poach on their preserves. But I want to give a few facts and figures to indicate the general magnitude of the expansion that has occurred.

During the past six years, the natural rate of increase of the Canadian population has been high and our numbers have been further enhanced by the accession of Newfoundland and by a large net immigration. Our national output in 1952 in terms of physical volume, was one quarter larger than in 1946 and almost double what it was just before the war in 1939. Another significant measure of Canada's economic growth is the proportion of our output devoted to capital investment—that is, additions to plant and equipment, new construction, development of new resources and other additions to productive capacity. Since the war we have been making very large outlays for new capital investment. They have been rising from year to year until last year in 1952 they totalled very nearly a quarter of our total national output. This is a very high percentage not only in comparison with most other countries but even in comparison with the United States where the figure is also high. A substantial part of this investment in Canada has gone into the development of natural resources, particularly oil and gas, iron ore, pulp and paper and a wide range of metals. But we have also been steadily expanding our industrial capacity and our power and transport facilities. Our economy is going through a period of rapid but balanced growth on many fronts rather than a violent, narrowly-based boom.

Has the expansion of the Canadian economy during the past few years automatically strengthened our balance of international payments and so raised the foreign exchange value of the Canadian dollar? Surprisingly enough, I think the answer is no: the Canadian dollar has risen not so much because of, as *in spite of,* the fact that our productive capacity is expanding at an extremely rapid rate. In most past periods of rapid economic expansion Canada has had a weak balance of payments on current account. We imported more goods and services from abroad than we were able to pay for out of our earnings abroad through exports of goods and services. We covered the balance by importing capital from outside Canada. Indeed, that is the natural situation for a new and growing country. Without the additional imports of goods and services that foreign capital makes possible, a young country would have to depend entirely on its own output to meet its needs. The more of its output it used to build new factories, power plants, oil refineries, and so on, the less would be available to meet the current consumption requirements of the people. On the other hand access to foreign capital enables a young country either to expand faster, or to live better while it is expanding, than would otherwise be possible.

It is a rather astonishing fact, therefore, that both in 1952, and over the post-war period as a whole, Canada has devoted a very high proportion of its output to the expansion of its productive capacity without, on balance, importing capital from outside Canada. The words "on balance" are important, for it has to be remembered that capital flows out of Canada as well as into Canada, though the outflows normally take a somewhat different form than the inflows. In 1952, for example, we received well over five hundred million dollars of long-term capital, mainly from the United States, either for direct investment in Canada or for the purchase of new securities issued by Canadian corporations and public bodies. These capital inflows have played an important part in helping to develop our resources. Joined to the money has been enterprise, imagination and know-how, and a willingness to take risks and the long view.

Valuable and important as these long-term capital inflows were, however, it still remains true that in the year 1952 they were more than fully offset by capital outflows of various kinds, mainly of a short-term character, so that on balance last year Canada was actually exporting capital on a small scale. During 1952 these capital outflows took such forms as the repurchase by Canadians of

Canadian securities held abroad, the building up of foreign currency balances abroad on the part of Canadians, and various other types of short-term capital outflow connected with foreign commerce. It is interesting to note in passing that these outflows occurred mainly in response to the rise in the exchange rate. The higher the rate went, the stronger became the incentives for these adjusting short-term capital movements. Indeed, this was probably the principal mechanism by which the demand for, and the supply of, Canadian dollars were brought into balance on the exchange market last year.

I have said that for the post-war period as a whole the sums Canadians invested, loaned or repaid abroad, i.e., our export of capital, more than offset the total inflow of capital into Canada from other countries. In other words, since the end of the war the savings needed to finance Canada's economic development have been provided from within the country itself on an overall basis.

I have pointed out that during 1952 this strength of the Canadian dollar was not, in fact, based on any net inflow of capital into Canada. On the contrary, we lived well within our current international income, spending about $150 million less on imports of goods and services from other countries than we earned from exports of goods and services. I have also pointed out that we managed to do this in spite of the large proportion of our output that we were devoting to the expansion of productive capacity rather than to current consumption. During this same period, we have managed to devote very substantial resources to our own defence programme and to contributions of defence equipment to our allies, without asking for or receiving mutual aid from the United States. How is it that we have lived within our international earnings and continued to have a strong dollar in spite of these claims on our economy?

The answer lies partly in good luck and partly, one would like to think, in the hard work and good management of Canadians. The high level of employment and incomes in the United States and other countries has been fortunate for us, because it has meant a very brisk demand for our exports, especially the basic foodstuffs and essential raw materials which we produce cheaply and abundantly. We have also been lucky in our last two grain crops, which have been exceptionally large, and which have come at a time when there was a very heavy demand for grain overseas. Finally, we have been lucky in that the prices of the things we import have fallen substantially, on balance, while the prices of the things we export have declined only slightly.

One would like to think, however, that Canadians have also had something to do with the strength of our balance of payments position in 1952 and indeed throughout the whole period. In recent years we have progressively moved towards more liberal economic arrangements until to-day we have no foreign exchange controls, no direct restrictions on imports, and a level of tariffs which has been substantially reduced since the mid-1930's.

In the absence of direct controls the main instruments for the general handling of our domestic situation have been fiscal and monetary policies. In every year since the war, we have achieved a budgetary surplus, notwithstanding the enormous growth of public expenditures on defence and on such social security measures as family allowances and old age pensions. When the economy was subjected to the world wide forces of inflation after Korea, reliance was placed on strict fiscal and monetary policies to keep inflation in check and safeguard our balance of payments position. The purpose generally was to avoid encouraging inefficient high-cost production and to keep the economy flexible so that business men could make their own adjustments to changing situations.

I hope that what I have said has contributed something to an understanding of the recent strength of the Canadian dollar over the last couple of years. The strength of the American dollar is often associated with the size of the American economy and its great productivity, with its high standard of living, and the fact that the United States can produce so many things much more cheaply than other countries can do. Canada's situation differs in many important respects from that of the United States.

We are, after all, a nation of fewer than fifteen million people living on the southern fringes of a vast sub-arctic area. It is true that we have valuable and substantial natural resources, but they are not nearly so varied or accessible as those of the United States. Man for man, our working force is not nearly so well provided with machinery and capital equipment. Consequently, the United States still out-produces Canada very substantially on a per capita basis: in 1952 our national output per head was about $1600, while that of the United States was about $2200. And on account of the sparseness of our population and the difficult physical characteristics of our country, the overhead costs involved in simply keeping the economy going weigh proportionately much more heavily on Canada than they do on the United States. There is, therefore, an even greater difference than the figures which I quoted would suggest between the output really available to Canadians and Americans to dispose of as they choose.

The relative smallness of our market and the rather specialized character of our resources make us much more dependent on foreign trade than the United States. If we were foolish enough to try to be self-sufficient, we could only do so with the greatest difficulty and at the cost of a very substantial reduction in our standard of living. Instead, we have learned to make the best of our situation by concentrating on the production for export of the things we can produce most efficiently and using the proceeds to buy from other countries the things we would find it very expensive to produce ourselves. This is reflected in the fact that we exported over 24 per cent of our national output in 1952 and spent a corresponding percentage of our national outlay on imports of goods and services. The comparable figures for the United States were only 5 per cent for exports and 4 per cent for imports.

Because of our great dependence on foreign trade we are vitally affected by developments outside Canada. We have very important economic ties not only with the United States but also with the United Kingdom and other sterling area countries, with Western Europe and with Latin America. We are vitally interested in the maintenance of a high level of economic activity in the United States and elsewhere. We are anxious to see liberal commercial and financial policies applied by major trading countries. Though trade between Canada and the United States is by no means free of restriction, it reached the very impressive figure of well over $5 billion last year. We bought goods from the United States worth about $3 billion and the United States bought goods from us worth $2.3 billion. This large two-way trade enables each country not only to enjoy a profitable market for its exports but also to obtain valuable imports more cheaply than it could produce them itself.

It will be obvious from what I have said about the importance of foreign trade to Canada that Canadians realize that their prosperity is intimately bound up with the prosperity of other people. Since the end of the war, financial assistance on an unprecedented scale from the United States (and on a smaller but proportionate scale from Canada) has helped in the recovery of our friends abroad and has helped maintain world trade at higher levels than would otherwise have been possible. The process of achieving international balance through massive injections of financial aid by the United States and by means of import restrictions and discrimination abroad obviously cannot go on for ever, and our friends abroad are anxious to stand on their own feet and to balance their international accounts through their own competitive efforts—that is, through increasing their dollar earnings. We in Canada would like to see them do this, not only because of our interests as a trading nation, but also because there is ample evidence that the alternative—of trying to achieve balance through import restrictions and discrimination—weakens the economic structure of the free world, and is damaging both to the restricting country and to the country whose exports are restricted. To achieve balance through an increase in dollar earnings requires that the countries now short of dollars pursue policies which make their export goods available at competitive prices. It also requires that American commercial policies be of a character which permits competition to result in foreign countries increasing their earnings of the dollars they need to pay for American exports. The responsibility for maintaining a high level of world trade, with the efficient use of economic resources from which we all benefit, is clearly one which is shared by all countries. This fact has been increasingly recognized, and it may well be the case that the chances of making substantial progress towards more liberal trading and currency arrangements are now more promising than they have been for many years. A fresh constructive effort along these lines would be warmly supported by Canada.

TAXES IN CANADA

Mr. J. H. Perry is Director of Research of the Canadian Tax Foundation, Toronto. From 1936 to 1952 he was with the Department of Finance of the federal government where, among other duties, he helped to advise the Minister of Finance on matters of taxation.

IV

TAXES IN CANADA

IN A THUMB-NAIL presentation of Canadian taxes two aspects demand priority. First, the facts; second, the philosophy.

The first fact is disillusioning. Despite recurrent reports in the press to the contrary, Canada is not a tax haven. This impression is probably due to the prominence given stories of Canadian tax *reductions*, as compared with the relative neglect of Canadian tax *increases*.

In actual fact the latest available data indicate that about the same proportion of national income, almost 30 per cent, is going into taxes in both Canada and the United States.

The second fact is inevitable in these troubled times. The cost of defence preparation is now the dominant element in Canadian government finance. As in the United States, roughly three-quarters of tax collections go to the national government. The dominant factor in the national budget in Canada, as in the United States, is defence. The Canadian defence bill in 1953 will account for more than 40 per cent of total federal expenditures, and it looks increasingly as though Canada is in defence spending to stay. As a result her federal budget will have to be maintained for some time at almost double its expected post-war level.

The third fact is the astonishingly good financial record of Canada in recent years. The extraordinary growth of the national tax base, combined with a degree of restraint in federal expenditures, has produced surpluses in each of the last seven years. As a result the federal debt has been reduced by 17 per cent in the post-war period. Even more striking is the reduction of 31 per cent in *per capita* federal debt.

These surpluses were the result partly of accident, partly of design. They were accidental to the extent that the effect on government revenues of the investment boom and the price inflation was not fully anticipated in projecting the annual budget

37

estimate. They were intentional to the extent that they represented the fulfilment of the announced purpose of the government after the war to retire as much debt as possible while the going was good.

On the whole, post-war government spending has been restrained. The considerable growth in the federal budget has been largely attributable to the defence programme and to the introduction of such social welfare measures as family allowances and old age pensions, which are supported by all parties. Allegations of waste in the defence programme are made as frequently in Canada as in the United States. But public discussion runs mainly in terms of petty thievery of service supplies. The real issue as to whether half of what Canada is spending might be too much, or twice what she is spending too little, seldom appears in discussions of waste in defence.

The fourth fact is that the Canadian tax structure of 1953, while a long way short of ideal perfection, is remarkably efficient and well-balanced. Some actual details will help to demonstrate this point.

The three main federal sources of revenue today are the corporation income tax, the personal income tax, and the 10 per cent manufacturers' sales tax. In addition there are heavy special taxes on liquor and tobacco, special excises, mainly at a 15 per cent rate, on automobiles, radios, television sets, soft drinks, candy, cosmetics, luggage, etc. The only other sizable revenue sources are the tariff and death duties. There is no excess profits tax and no tax on capital gains.

To elaborate briefly, since the recent budget the corporation income tax in Canada is 18 per cent on the first $20,000 of profits, and 47 per cent on the balance. In addition there is a 2 per cent tax for old age security, so that the total rates are 20 per cent and 49 per cent respectively. Personal income tax rates are lower and exemptions are higher than in the United States, and, except for the income-splitting privilege allowed married persons, practically all Canadian tax-payers would pay less than their American counterparts.

The notable difference, indeed the essential difference, in the two federal revenue systems is the Canadian 10 per cent manufacturers' sales tax.

Provincial and municipal tax systems in Canada correspond generally to state and local systems in the United States. Some very significant contrasts do arise, however, out of the present allocation of tax sources between the federal and provincial governments. In particular the following points are important:

First, there is only one personal income tax in Canada, the federal levy.

Second, there are only two corporation income taxes in Canada, the federal levy and that of the province of Quebec.

Third, there are only three death taxes, the federal and those of Ontario and Quebec.

This happy and unusual state of affairs is attributable to what are known in Canada as the Tax Rental Agreements. Under these agreements all provinces but Quebec have undertaken not to impose personal or corporation income taxes or death duties for the five years 1952 to 1956 inclusive. The one modification that must be made to this statement is that Ontario has retained its right to collect death duties, an option available to any province under the terms of the agreements. Substantial grants are made by the federal government in return for these provincial undertakings.

So much for some of the salient *facts* concerning taxation in Canada in 1953. What then can be said of the present Canadian tax philosophy?

First, concerted efforts to improve the revenue laws and tax administration at the federal level in the post-war period give unmistakable evidence of a philosophy of less complicated tax compliance and improved revenue collection. Laws have been redrafted, administrative procedures streamlined, forms simplified, nuisance taxes repealed and in many other ways the tax system has undergone marked improvement. These changes have not loosened the harness, but they have removed several sore spots where it was rubbing.

Second, the philosophy of efficiency in taxation has also been the keynote of the Tax Rental Agreements. These have proved that internal tax arrangements between levels of government need not be chaotic. They have also demonstrated that much more can be achieved by centralized administration and inter-governmental grants, without loss of autonomy or infringement of "state rights", than has been assumed in the past.

Third, in Canada the income tax has been taken off its pedestal as the perfect fiscal device. Indirect taxes, such as our general sales tax, are used in order to obtain revenue from income levels where direct taxation is not feasible and in order to avoid pressing the income tax to the point where its grossest defects become intolerable. In the opinion of tax authorities such indirect taxation as the general sales tax is not only efficient and productive, but also meets the test of fairness. This attitude can be summed up by saying that more stress is placed on the merits of a well-balanced tax structure than on one which relies heavily on taxes which are perfect in theory but which in practice reveal very serious weaknesses.

Fourth, the tax system is now used in Canada as a dynamic factor in the economy. Post-war years reveal several remarkable experiments in the use of taxation for purposes of economic control. This has been particularly characteristic of the defence period. Fiscal and monetary measures, supplemented by a minimum of direct control, have been heavily relied upon to absorb the major shock of defence spending on the economy. The government has felt it preferable to make the adjustment to a defence economy, and it has been successfully made, by altering the conditions in which the economy operates rather than by interfering directly with its operation. By way of illustration, despite concerted pressure from several directions, price control has not been re-introduced in the defence build-up period.

Finally, despite the occasional rude jolts to the business community as a result of the use of taxation for economic control purposes, the underlying post-war philosophy has been that business deserves a break. This has been demonstrated so repeatedly that a complete list of individual instances would be an extremely long one. Perhaps the most outstanding has been the refusal of the government to impose an excess profits tax in the defence period. Another illustration is the recent budget, in which revenue was surrendered by granting tax reductions for business, reductions which would have attracted much more political favour if given in other directions. Here is a practical instance from this budget. The dividend received credit was increased to 20 per cent, and the low bracket rate of corporation income tax was simultaneously set at 20 per cent on the first $20,000 of income. The result is that for three-quarters of the corporations, the "small businesses", double taxation has been completely removed. In the same budget the

Minister of Finance fulfilled his oft-repeated desire to bring the corporation tax rate below 50 per cent.

These changes, which appear to favour business, represent neither the political caprice of a government facing an election nor callous disregard for modern enlightened views of social justice. Indeed the true genius of Canadian fiscal policy today lies in the skill with which the gradual progress of the welfare state is being harmonized with continuous and accelerating growth in a free economy.

LABOUR RELATIONS

Mr. Patrick Conroy is at present Labour Attaché at the Canadian Embassy in Washington. He came to Canada at the age of nineteen, after six years experience in the Scottish coal mines. He was active in the United Mine Workers of America and was subsequently appointed Secretary-Treasurer of the Canadian Congress of Labour.

V

LABOUR RELATIONS

WITHIN THE LAST FEW YEARS Canada has been the subject of much comment and speculation, both centred largely upon her industrial expansion since the end of World War II. This expansion has been substantial and has been assessed largely in terms of dollar investments. As investment has increased from year to year, speculations as to Canada's future have grown accordingly. Most of what has been said about our country has been very favourable. Flattery is pleasant and, perhaps, necessary for all of us, but only for the moment. It is a heady wine and can have a very dangerous effect not only on the individual but on a people as well. Canada has been imbibing as much wine as it can absorb for the moment without losing its balance or sense of proportion. Give us too much praise and we can become something of a problem both to ourselves and to our neighbours. Canadians ought to take a holiday from believing all the complimentary things that have been said and take a sober look at what has been happening in Canada in recent years.

An objective appraisal of Canada's notable industrial expansion means much more than a continuing assessment of the billions of dollars that are being invested in her national development. Such investment and development are both good and creditable in themselves, but of themselves and by themselves mean literally nothing.

At best, monetary investment, resource development, and plant erection are but the beginning of a process. The end of that process is the effect that investment and development have on Canada and how they are affecting our people. This is the test. Where can we find the answer to this question? Investment and accruing development mean production which, in turn, symbolizes people working together. Those who work together in this field are called respectively management and labour. Their day to day association has come to be known as labour relations. Labour relations are, of course, basically human relations and if we can find out what is happening in these relations, we know fairly accurately whether the current expansion in Canada is proving to be a good thing or otherwise for our country.

Labour relations in Canada are on the whole reasonably good. Emphasis should be placed on the reference "reasonably" because the answer to this question must be kept within the bounds of reason. There is neither point nor sense in casting a luring eye at the investor with the slot-machine or jack-pot mentality, nor, on the other hand, at the fellow who seeks to establish trouble as the yardstick of normal human behaviour.

Our labour relations in Canada are almost parallel to the country's contemporary industrial development. They really started in 1939, when Canada entered World War II, although it is true that we had several generations of relationships between employers and unions before then. Canada's early industrial history was largely a record of rather haphazard relationships, a tug-of-war, with the strong conquering the weak. There was, however, a sequence of historical highlights. Following Confederation in 1867 unions were relieved of the burden of being regarded as a conspiracy against and in restraint of trade. In the first decade of this century the foundations were laid of our existing machinery for conciliation of disputes. The late William Lyon Mackenzie King, Prime Minister of Canada for so many years, was the chief architect and advocate of such machinery. In the middle twenties and thirties several of the provinces passed permissive legislation that claimed to give unions the right to organize. It was not, however, until World War II that Canada, on a national basis, began to adopt policies that would translate industrial relationships into something approaching a civilized process.

The reasons for paying new attention to this area of human behaviour were not strictly humanitarian. It was found impossible to engage successfully in a modern war, with all its demands, while at the same time enjoying the doubtful luxury of having the country torn apart in industrial warfare. Something had to be done. In the year 1940 the federal government passed what might again be called "permissive legislation" that said, in effect, that unions had the right to organize and bargain collectively with employers. To a point this permissive legislation, coupled with conciliation machinery, served a purpose. Some employers accepted the legislation as a matter of national policy. Others did not, and in the middle of the war Canada had to recast its labour legislation. The new legislation was of an emergency nature designed for the war period only. It covered all industries relating to war production and made collective bargaining mandatory. The provinces also adjusted their legislation to cover purely provincial jurisdiction. In both areas, federal and provincial, the legislation, supplemented by Wage Boards to deal with the wage question and buttressed by conciliation machinery, worked reasonably well. The war ended and with the beginning of peace the whole question had to be reconsidered.

Normally, with the exception of purely federal industries and undertakings, the bulk of Canadian labour jurisdiction is in the hands of the provinces. The provinces are most insistent on retaining their constitutional rights in this field.

Immediately after the war the federal government drafted a peace time labour code. Before doing so, the government consulted all parties having to do with labour relations, employers, unions, the provinces, and individuals with a knowledge of that field. The proposed new legislation was drafted on the basis of our previous experience. After a period of some months, during which the provinces and interested parties were examining the draft legislation, a federal-provincial conference was called to put the pieces together and complete the first peace time country-wide legislation. The outcome of this conference was the National Labour Statute. It was frankly a compromise. Labour thought that it was inadequate and not enough. Employers thought that it gave too much to labour. Some provinces thought that the new medicine was too strong, others that it was too weak. Certainly it was no new wonder drug nor a curative for every ill in the field of human relations.

The new legislation was designed for practical purposes. First of all, it covered only federal jurisdiction, which, in Canada, is limited to railways, communications, dockyards and certain federally owned projects. At least 75 per cent of Canadian labour jurisdiction lies with provincial authority. The new federal Act, therefore, became the basis upon which all provincial legislation was built. Some provinces went farther. Others did not go quite so far.

The principles, however, of all the legislation, both federal and provincial, are of a pattern and function on a similar basis. Our legislation is comparatively simple and provides for the following:

1. The right to organize and bargain collectively.
2. Action against unfair labour practices.
3. A clause in each collective agreement to arbitrate the settlement of disputes within the life of an agreement.
4. A minimum period for any collective agreement.
5. Decertification of unions no longer representing the majority of workers in a plant or establishment.

All of the legislation, both on the federal and provincial levels, makes specific provision for conciliation and settlement of disputes.

The fundamentals of our conciliation machinery have not changed in over forty years. In fact it is out of that forty years' experience that the conciliation machinery maintains itself. This machinery is simple. It is designed to prevent strikes and trouble and is, in effect, preventive. How does it work? Both federal and provincial governments watch the industrial field. If an employer and union cannot agree, government conciliators inject themselves into the dispute and attempt a settlement. Their approach is strictly non-partisan and their purpose objective in trying to bring about a satisfactory settlement between the parties. Conciliators quite definitely steer clear of supporting one party or the other. Should the efforts of the conciliators be unsuccessful, either party has the right to apply for the setting up of a board of conciliation and investigation. If the government is satisfied that the parties in dispute have exhausted their resources and cannot reach an agreement, it proceeds to notify the employer and the union that a board of conciliation will be appointed. The union and employer are each asked to nominate a person to represent them on the board. Having done so, the two parties are then requested to confer together with a view to selecting a chairman for the board. If they agree on a chairman, they notify the Minister of Labour, who then advises the new chairman and representatives to have the board get under way. Should the two parties be unable to agree upon a chairman, the Minister himself then makes the appointment. The board attempts first to conciliate the dispute. Failing conciliation, it then proceeds to investigate, takes evidence, and finally makes recommendations for a settlement. In the federal field, from the beginning of conciliation procedures until seven days after the board of conciliation makes its report, strikes and lockouts are prohibited and the *status quo* in working conditions and wages must be maintained. Different provinces have varying periods of grace following the report of a board. In addition the board's report forms the basis of subsequent negotiations between the parties, during which time government conciliators may again sit in with the parties to assist in arriving at a settlement.

We now come to an accounting of our collective bargaining legislation and conciliation machinery. Under test how has it worked out? Does our machinery help in maintaining a maximum of industrial peace? The answer is yes. The 1952 record showed that:

(a) There were some 7,000 collective bargaining contracts in effect throughout the length and breadth of Canada.

(b) Out of 7,000 collective agreements, some 4,900 contracts were settled or renewed peacefully between the parties on a voluntary basis.

(c) The total number of cases applying for the use of government conciliation machinery was 2,089.

A summary for 1952 shows that out of 7,000 agreements in force, some 6,775 were settled peacefully either by voluntary negotiation or through a process of governmental conciliation. Out of 7,000 agreements, there was a total of 222 strikes. Sixty-nine strikes ensued because of the inability of conciliation people to bring enough reason to bear on a settlement, while 153 strikes took place for a variety of causes and where no conciliation efforts had been applied or asked for. The performance in 1952, therefore, indicates that 97 per cent of the collective agreements were negotiated peacefully and without strikes, while only 3 per cent were involved in the strike process. We have enough hardihood to think this is a creditable performance, achieved by labour, employers and governments working hand in hand to maintain industrial peace.

What has been the effect of labour legislation on the unions? Since 1940 the numbers in the trade union movement have more than trebled. What is the effect on business? No major business has suffered. If any small business has suffered, the casualties have not yet been brought to light. The fact that Canada is now being cited and pointed to as a land of comparative milk and honey would seem to be a sufficient answer to this question. What does labour think of the legislation? Generally labour believes that the legislation could be improved. What do employers think of the legislation? Many employers believe that labour is becoming too strong under the legislation and they would like to insert some safeguards to protect their interests. What are the main complaints against the legislation? The chief complaints are largely against our conciliation machinery. For the most part the unions make the allegation that our conciliation procedures take too long. There is probably some justification for this charge, but the justification must be qualified. At times those complaining about the delay are themselves the chief sinners in holding up a settlement and this applies to both unions and employers.

Supplementing our collective bargaining and conciliation machinery, the federal government sponsors a Labour-Management Co-operative Production Service with the stated purpose of using every legitimate method to increase production. This Service, started during the war and continued in the post-war period, has resulted in the setting up of approximately nine hundred Labour-Management Production Plant Committees throughout Canada. The Committees deal with all matters pertaining to production and in no way impinge on the collective bargaining process. The idea behind these Committees is to establish a permanent day-to-day means of communication between workers and employers and build up a maximum pool of goodwill from this relationship. The work is slow, but on the whole the results have been good. We have many testimonials from both management and labour that the proper functioning of these joint Plant Committees has proved to be a leavening process that helps both parties engaged in production.

Figures, of course, cannot tell the whole story of labour relations. What would be a reasonable assessment of the results of our legislation and its bearing on the economy? There are, of course, exceptions where abuses, and sometimes very flagrant ones, take place. No one area can be cited as being more virtuous than another. Some employers are still thinking in terms of 1853 rather than in the twentieth century. They do not want unions and will do their best to destroy them. On the other side of the fence some unions feel that the best way to be agreeable is by being disagreeable. On both sides, however, the parties are showing increasing evidence of maturity and an awareness that since they have to live together, ways and means can be found to make life tolerable for both.

The greatest possible emphasis must be laid on voluntary settlement. The boards of conciliation are used as mechanisms to make it possible for the parties to reach voluntary agreement, which finally they have to do. This is agreement by "consent of the governed". Such an approach, therefore, rules out arbitration as a permanent substitute for voluntary collective bargaining. Here and there in some provinces arbitration is used in settling disputes in the public service, but even there the parties are not too happy about it in their particular localities. The regimentation implied in arbitration would seem opposed to the growth of responsible citizenship. One or two instances of arbitration have occurred in cases of emergency. Neither party was too satisfied with the results. A cross section of business and labour is against arbitration as offering neither a panacea nor a permanent yard-stick for settling industrial disputes. The government's view of existing legislation is that while it may not be perfect, it comes fairly close to being satisfactory. Not many have suffered from its operations. The policy of the government in this field has had two objectives in view. One has been to lay a foundation that can be built upon in the light of experience. The other has been to avoid legislation of one extreme or the other in the belief that an unbalance in one direction inevitably produces extremes in another direction.

Human beings are not, of course, perfect. That is why Canadian labour legislation and labour relations are still some distance away from perfection. This, however, can be said. Anyone, whether on the labour side or the employer side, who wants to play the game in the light of the general good will find a greater area of response today in Canada than at any time in her history. Despite the exceptions on both sides and despite the charges and counter charges which have become common usage between management and unions, both are getting along better. Perhaps the improvement is in spite of themselves, but the record does show an improvement. Canadians are not a spectacular people. They are, perhaps, on the conservative side, but on the whole they are a fairly reasonable and proud people. We welcome strangers coming to our country, but we do want to welcome the civilized person who knows that money is not an end in itself but that its wise use can produce a growing number of people of greater stature who can be respected as equal partners in that vital and controversial field called labour relations.

Department of Resources and Development

HIGHWAY BUILDING IN CANADA

In the world outside, Canadians have the reputation for being cautious or even over-cautious. In fact, however, the opposite is true. The extension of boundaries, the building of roads and railways, have always tended in Canada's history to outrun the limits of settlement.

THE MAIN DAM AT DES JOACHIMS

Canada abounds with lakes and rivers. We are constantly pushing back our northern frontiers, using water to turn the wheels of industry and to light the cities.

SOCIAL LEGISLATION

Mrs. Adelaide Sinclair is Executive Assistant to the Deputy Minister of Welfare in the Department of National Health and Welfare. Since 1947 she has been Canadian delegate to the United Nations International Children's Emergency Fund and for three successive years was Chairman of the Programme Committee and for two years Chairman of the Executive Board. She has represented Canada at UNESCO and was Alternate Delegate to the United Nations in 1950.

VI

SOCIAL LEGISLATION

SOCIAL LEGISLATION is capable of very wide definitions and to deal with it in one chapter we have to confine ourselves within reasonable limits. Perhaps the most useful thing to do is confine the discussion to those programmes in which Canadian governments, either federal or provincial, have undertaken to give direct financial aid to certain groups, such as the unemployed, the aged, the disabled. It should be made quite clear, however, that that is not by any means the only social legislation that there is in Canada. There is a long tradition of social services of various kinds which originated before the newer governmental techniques and which also contribute a great deal to the welfare of the people.

Most western industrial countries have some forms of social legislation. These have grown up because with every industrial economy there have arisen a good many hazards or contingencies which leave the individual citizen somewhat helpless if he falls a victim to them. He cannot provide for all of them and by degrees society has recognized that it has some responsibility in providing for at least the percentage of its population that may be subject to these contingencies. For instance we learned in the 'thirties that willingness to work was not in itself a guarantee that one could find employment. We cannot eliminate all industrial accidents and the statisticians assure us that more and more of us are going to live longer after we retire. Because of Canada's fairly recent industrialization, she has had an opportunity to look at what has happened in a number of other countries and to make plans on the basis of other people's experience, and perhaps their mistakes, and to select what seemed best. It would be an easier task to discuss Canadian social legislation if it was all cut from one pattern and came in a nice neat package. Unfortunately that is not the case. Perhaps it is true to say that Canadians feel no philosophic urge to do things in tidy packages. We tend to meet problems as they arise and to find the solution which seems best at that moment. In another decade we might think differently, conditions might be different, and we might produce different solutions to similar problems. Consequently you find that examples of almost every known type of social legislation have found their way into Canada's statute books in the last thirty-five years. We still have a number of problems we have not solved and we are looking for ways to solve them. At the present time we have made provision for certain benefits for children, for old people, for the unemployed, and for certain groups of sick and disabled citizens, such as the blind. We have done this in a great variety of ways. Some of them are financed by the federal government, some by provincial governments, and some by both together. Some are given to everybody without any contributions, some are given only on proof of need for the particular service that is required. Here, perhaps, a definition should be given of a phrase that is very often used in Canada, and that is programmes based on a "means test." That simply means that you have to prove that your means are below a certain level before you qualify for certain benefits.

Under a federal form of government certain constitutional and jurisdictional problems arise which are sometimes a little hard to explain to people who do not live under them, but these have coloured to some extent the social legislation in Canada. When the Canadian provinces united in 1867, no social legislation in today's sense had been thought of and there was no clear provision that the federal government had any jurisdiction in that field at all. That is quite understandable because at that time social need, relief, charity, or whatever it was called in those days, was considered very local, a very personal and parochial problem, and national governments had taken very little part in it. It did mean certain problems later on. When you begin to get into this field of social legislation, you find its first manifestations in Canada at the provincial level, but what you also notice, as the story goes on, is that there is an increasing trend to bring the federal government in to a larger and larger participation. The explanation, very briefly, is that as the country developed, it became quite evident that the wealth was rather unevenly distributed among the provinces and that if a large national financial provision was needed for any contingency, the federal treasury was the only one with sufficient taxing powers and sufficient resources to provide it. Consequently there has been an increasing tendency, as the programmes developed, for the federal government to assume more and more share in large economic maintenance programmes and to leave to the provinces and the local authorities the spheres where local administration, local knowledge and personal services are required.

The first two programmes that should be mentioned very briefly were provincial ones. The very first was the Workmen's Compensation Act, which was passed in Ontario in 1915. We now have this type of legislation in all our provinces. It provides for a fund to which employers only, in certain specified industries, contribute and which is administered by boards set up by the provinces to compensate employees for industrial accident or illness. The other provincial programme was introduced first in 1916 in the province of Manitoba and that was the Mothers' Allowance Act. That has now been adopted in all other provinces. There are slight provincial variations but it is basically the same programme. It is to provide for mothers who for one reason or another are left with dependent children with no means of support. The father may have died, he may have deserted, he may have become disabled, he may have gone to jail, or there may be a variety of other causes, but in any case he is no longer supporting his family, and the mother is faced with the problem of going out to earn a living and perhaps breaking up the home and putting the children either in institutions or elsewhere. In order to prevent this and if possible to keep the home together, if she can establish that she has no means to do this, she is given an allowance for herself and a certain amount for each child, so that she may keep the home together and keep the children in it. This begins to show signs of what is characteristic of a good many of Canadian programmes, a mixture of humanitarian and economic considerations. Obviously humanity would suggest that you do something for the mother and the children. It is sound social practice to keep them at home, if you can. It is also very much less expensive to pay the mother to keep them in the home than to pay board for the children in some other place.

Those were the early types of programme that grew up in the provinces and while those were developing, there was very little acceptance of any federal responsibility in the social field. But after the first war, when thinking began to change, the federal government found itself providing a good deal of welfare for veterans, who were, of course, clearly their responsibility, and there began to be the feeling that perhaps the federal government should do more. The first manifestation of this in any concrete form came in the late 1920's, when the federal government made its first attempt to do something for the aged. There was an increasing number of indigent old people that was reaching proportions that private charity could not cope with, and that many of the municipalities could not cope with, and the federal government proposed to step in. Certain constitutional questions were raised as to whether the federal government had any right to set up a pensions programme of any kind and in order to avoid that difficulty, what was proposed in the Old Age Pensions Act of 1927 was a joint programme between the federal government and the provinces. It, like mothers' allowances, was basically a relief or public assistance programme. It was not a pension programme in the sense that anybody contributed to it as an individual in order to receive benefits. The proposal was that anybody who was seventy years of age and older and who had lived in Canada approximately twenty years, if their resources or their income were below a certain level, might apply for a pension. The legislation was permissive. The federal government simply said that if a province wanted to embark on a programme of this kind, they would pay half the pension. They could not force it, but they were prepared to reimburse the province. It went a little slowly at first and after a few years the federal government decided further inducements were necessary. The federal government offered to pay 75 per cent of the pensions and that proved sufficient. By 1938 all provinces in Canada had entered into agreements with the federal government and were paying these pensions. During this time they had also included pensions for blind persons in the same scheme.

It was not until the 'thirties that Canada began to look into the new area of social insurance and to bring in a regular insurance type of social legislation. The phase in which that was introduced was the unemployment insurance field. The 1930's had been a very difficult period. Relief had traditionally been a matter for the municipalities. A good many municipalities had been reduced almost to bankruptcy. Many provinces had felt that they were unequal to carrying the increasing burden by themselves and the federal government had been drawn into the relief payments to support the municipal and provincial grants. There was a tremendous strain on the whole economy and it left the country with the determination that if anything like this was ever going to happen again, it would at all costs be in some way prepared for it. Unemployment insurance seemed a suitable beginning. The government took a long hard look at what other countries had done in this field and finally decided that a federal programme of unemployment insurance would most satisfactorily meet the nation's needs. This did not follow the example of the United States, which has state programmes. Canada now has a federal unemployment scheme. It took a little while to persuade all the provinces that this authority and this prerogative should be turned over to the federal government, but in the end they agreed. It required a constitutional amendment to permit the federal government to enter into the field of unemployment insurance, but that was secured and the bill became law in 1940. It is a perfectly orthodox insurance scheme. A person's benefits relate to the contributions he has paid in. Employers and employees pay approximately equal contributions and the federal government contributes about one-fifth of their total and carries all the costs of administration. There has been high employment in Canada ever since that Act was passed and therefore the unemployment insurance fund today is in an extremely solvent condition.

Up to 1940, it is probably fair to say that Canadian programmes had been rather modest and traditional. That is considered a characteristic Canadian pattern. But either on account of the war, or for some other reason, Canadians became a good deal more independent in their thinking and certainly a good deal more venturesome in their planning. Most interesting perhaps are the two most recent pieces of legislation, the Family Allowances Act of 1944 and the Old Age Security Act of 1951. The Family Allowances Act is a purely federal measure. For the first time, under this Act, Canada adopted the principle of what is called "universality" and that means that it is not limited to the disabled or any particular group. In the Family Allowances Act the government undertakes to pay to the mother of every child born in Canada and every child who has lived there for a year, but was not born there, a monthly allowance. It is not a very large one. It runs from $5 to $8 a month, depending on the age of the child, and is payable up until the time of the child's sixteenth birthday. The funds come out of the general tax revenues. Nobody has to contribute to be eligible. Nobody has to establish that he needs this particular allowance. In February, 1953, Canada was paying allowances for 4,711,156 children at a monthly cost of over $28,000,000, which comes to an annual bill of about $330,000,000. What is significant about this particular Act is that it owes its origins quite as much to economic as to welfare considerations. In the chapters on the Canadian dollar and on Canadian taxation Family Allowances and Old Age Pensions are referred to in connection with fiscal policy. This must be borne in mind in order to understand the philosophy behind these programmes. When the war was drawing to a close, Canadian economists and financial advisers were very apprehensive that history would repeat itself and bring the same post-war depression that followed the first war. Canada had just come through the 'thirties and those lessons were fairly fresh. One step had just been taken in providing unemployment insurance. That was going to keep a certain amount of purchasing power in the hands of a certain number of people for a limited period of time and it was hoped that it would cushion any sort of depression that might follow. But it was not felt that that would be sufficient. In looking for other means for keeping up the community's purchasing power, the decision was taken to introduce this family allowance programme, which would keep purchasing power flowing in to Canadian homes with children, in every nook and cranny of the country every month, and which would serve to put a very modest, but certainly some, little floor under consumers' spendings. There were people, of course, who were much more interested in it from the welfare aspects, for the effect that it was going to have on the care and the standard of living of children, particularly for the less privileged group. There was also a feeling that it compensated for the fact that under Canada's wage structure wages are paid regardless of family responsibilities. The whole community now contributes to that particularly heavy period when children are under sixteen.

One thing that surprised nearly everyone who was interested

in this was the very small amount of opposition there was to this new proposal, which was a very new and radical and expensive one. The Act was passed quite quickly and has equally quickly become an accepted part of the country's social fabric. It is only fair to say that in the early days there were a few furious fathers who saw no reason that the cheque should be paid to the mothers, but few of them have pursued that matter very much further. Those responsible for the programme feel that the decision has been amply justified by the small amount of abuse that has been brought to their attention in the spending of these allowances. The mothers are primarily interested in the spending of them for the welfare of the children, which is the purpose for which they were intended. There are occasional protests that lazy parents are living in luxury and idleness on the family allowance cheques. This is reminiscent of the Wall Street Journal which recently took time to complain rather bitterly how Canada was demoralizing her noble Eskimos by paying a family allowance, which meant they stopped hunting and fishing and all the useful things they did and were sitting with their feet up drawing family allowance cheques. One of the big oil companies in the United States put a large advertisement in a weekly magazine not long ago telling rather the same story. In judging the accuracy of these tales, one need only consider that the allowances consist of from $5 to $8 a month per child, which is a maximum of $60 to $96 a year. At present prices one can hardly live in luxury and idleness on that.

One interesting outcome of this legislation was that welfare was recognized at the time of the passing of this Act as justifying a Cabinet position in the federal government and at that time a new Department of National Health and Welfare was set up in which were incorporated most of the existing health services, the responsibility for family allowances, for the federal part of the old age pensions programme, and later our Old Age Security Act. The unemployment insurance programme had been set up under the Department of Labour.

Following the war there were a good many complaints about the Old Age Pensions Act. Most of them were directed towards the means test, which was considered rather harsh and humiliating. The other complaints were against the fact that it did not begin until seventy years of age, which was considered too high. In order to meet these complaints the government in 1950 appointed a parliamentary committee. It represented all parties in both Houses and studied the question of what Canada should do about its old age security. That committee worked very seriously. It examined such things as the Old Age and Survivors' Insurance in the United States and the programmes in effect in the United Kingdom, Australia, New Zealand and the Scandinavian countries, and finally came up with a proposal for Canada which was not exactly like any of them, but did take into account the experience of other countries. That proposal was that once again the programme should be universal and that everybody in Canada seventy years of age and over who had lived in the country for twenty years should be paid forty dollars a month for the rest of their lives. There were, of course, a number of considerations that led to this, some of which have already been mentioned. One of the most important was the administrative simplicity of a programme of that kind compared to the complications of a strictly insurance scheme with individual contributions. The universality is demonstrated by the fact that the Prime Minister is drawing one of these old age pensions. He is qualified by age and residence.

The government was not prepared to pay universal pensions to people below the age of seventy, but it did recognize that between sixty-five and sixty-nine there were certain people who had real financial problems. They might have been under compulsory retirement at the age of sixty-five and have very few resources until they became eligible for the pension at seventy. What the government did in effect was to take the old type of means test programme and offer to pay the sixty-five to sixty-nine group on a means test basis, that is the people who really need it and who can prove, if not destitution, something approaching it. This will be continued on the basis of a joint programme with the provinces.

The federal government has indicated its willingness under certain conditions to share the cost of a health insurance plan with the provincial governments up to a fixed amount per capita, but no programme has been worked out yet. A first step, however, is the fact that since 1948 the federal government has given health grants to the provinces for a variety of purposes, such as the building of hospitals. Two provincial governments have passed compulsory hospital insurance laws and other local experiments are being watched carefully.

It should be emphasized that the legislation, which has been outlined very briefly, has been as much a part of the fiscal policy of Canada as it has been an expression of a desire for greater social justice, particularly in the case of the universal benefits, which have considerable effect on our purchasing power. The benefits under family allowances cost about $330,000,000 a year, for old age security very nearly $320,000,000 a year. From time to time calculations are made as to how much is spent on all the welfare programmes. The most recent calculation is that for the fiscal year 1952-53, taking the programmes mentioned and other welfare services, provincial, municipal and private, Canada will spend about one and a half billion dollars.

This may appear to be a rather mixed bag of social legislation. No attempt has been made to discuss the broader aspects of social welfare or social security, nor to suggest whether or not the sum of this legislation makes Canada a welfare state. The phrase "welfare state" seems to mean different things to different people. It is quite clear, however, that Canada's programmes are at least compatible with a balanced budget, with high employment, with expanding production and with increasing productivity. Canada has a pragmatic approach to its problems. It has not set its sights on any kind of formalized Utopia, but will probably go on trying to meet the needs of its citizens as those needs arise and as its resources permit. Canada's aim is well summed up in the words of Abraham Lincoln who said at one time that the function of government is to render services that people in their private capacities cannot provide for themselves or cannot provide as well as the government can.

GOVERNMENT AND BUSINESS

MR. JOHN T. BRYDEN is General Manager of the North American Life Assurance Company. He joined the Company in 1929 and was appointed General Manager in 1950. In 1940 Mr. Bryden was on loan to the Dominion Government preparing financial statistics for submission to the 1941 Dominion-Provincial Conference. He is a member of the Executive Council of the Canadian Chamber of Commerce.

VII

GOVERNMENT AND BUSINESS

> Both Canadian business and Canadian government have adopted
> and accepted the system of private competitive enterprise, and the
> support of that system is a basic and sufficient principle for the
> guidance of both members of this unique Canadian partnership.

THAT STATEMENT is taken from the most recent policy declarations of the Canadian Chamber of Commerce. Similar
sentiments were recently expressed by the Prime Minister, Mr. St.
Laurent, when he said: "The real justification of free enterprise
is that it provides a better life for more people than any other
kind of economic system." He added: "I don't think that free
enterprise requires that governments do nothing about economic
conditions. Governments can—and I believe governments should—
pursue fiscal and commercial policies which will encourage and
stimulate enterprise, and wise government policies can do a lot to
maintain the right kind of economic climate."

The attitudes of business and government toward one another
are of vital importance, and in Canada the existing relationship is
unique, valuable and worth keeping.

For instance, on January 20th last I was a member of the
Canadian Chamber of Commerce delegation which presented to
the government at Ottawa the Chamber's policy declarations and
resolutions. We were welcomed by the Prime Minister himself
and met with all the members of his Cabinet who were in Ottawa
that day. We had an opportunity of presenting the views of business
on many points and the benefit of discussion on some of them. That
kind of meeting is an annual occurrence and takes place before
government budget policy is established.

Later that day a smaller delegation presented to the Ministers
of Finance and National Revenue and key members of their
departments a brief on fiscal policy and specific recommendations

regarding the Income Tax Act and the Succession Duty Act. This presentation, of course, was much more detailed and productive of further discussion and exchange of views.

These illustrations are cited not to indicate that government always follows the recommendations of business. It is not so. They are cited, however, to indicate that the point of view of business on the matters of the day can be placed before those responsible for government policy decisions, and it does receive consideration. Such a method of operation fosters a degree of intimacy and informality that is desirable, and helps to create a feeling of partnership and mutual respect.

Much the same feeling exists between many business men and those responsible for government administration at the senior civil servant level, the Deputy Ministers and their assistants. Some of these men have had business experience. Nearly all of them worked with the many business men recruited during the last war for the special jobs and activities associated with price control, rationing, war industries control, foreign exchange control, war finance and so on. Those shared experiences in many cases built solid friendships and a mutual respect which is part and parcel of the government-business relationship in Canada.

With regard to government supervision of existing statutes, life insurance is perhaps one of the best examples of competitive enterprise operating within a framework of sane insurance laws and sound government supervision. There has been a Department of Insurance at the federal level since 1875. Annual reports to this Department are detailed and comprehensive. To this supervision must be given part of the credit for the standing and reputation of the Canadian life insurance companies, for the fact that no policyholder in a Canadian life insurance Company has ever lost a dollar through non-payment of the amount guaranteed to him under his contract either at death or on maturity, and for the reception accorded Canadian life insurance companies in the United States and in the sixty odd other countries where they have business in force.

It would be wrong to conclude, however, that business and government are always in accord. There are differences of opinion with government and, from time to time, sharp differences, on the individual company level, on the industry level and on the whole

BELL ISLAND, MINING, NEWFOUNDLAND

The great natural resources of land, of water falls, of forests and rocks, are resources which are recognized as assets today but were regarded as barriers by our forebears. They became assets only when Canadians learned how to use them.

CANADA'S OLDEST INDUSTRY

Fur trapping, which was Canada's first industry and which was responsible for much of the exploration of the land, is still of importance to the Canadian economy.

business community level. Sometimes business speaks with one voice; sometimes with several. Then trade associations or individual companies urge their separate views. This is evidence of a healthy situation. It does, however, make it difficult for any one business man to deal adequately with the subject of "the point of view of business."

Canada, in common with other countries, has not been immune over the last two decades to the trend towards economic and social planning, which has been inherent in the general acceptance of the philosophy of full employment. Implementation of such a philosophy has led to much more active direction and stimulation by government of the economic processes and in many cases extension of governmental activity to achieve some economic or social objective.

Business has been opposed to the extension of governmental intervention beyond the point where there is a clear need to protect some accurately defined public interest. Of course, business and government have not always seen eye to eye on the definition of "public interest" nor on the establishment of "clear need."

There are examples of government ownership. Some have been by accident. For instance, the Canadian National Railway system was the outcome of some very widespread bankruptcies in the 'twenties. Today it competes with the Canadian Pacific Railway, a private carrier. Others have been by design. Our Canadian Broadcasting Corporation and Trans-Canada Airlines both enjoy government monopolies. Private competition is strictly controlled in the main areas in which they operate. Public ownership of some hydro power utilities has been spurred by tax differentials. Crown agencies are identified with atomic energy, synthetic rubber and housing. All of these are the subject of lively debate. Despite these examples, however, it would be fair to say that government in Canada has not gone nearly as far as it might have gone in the direction of imposing and maintaining controls and in the amount of government intervention and ownership, had its basic philosophy not been one of a preference for the maintenance of a wide area of freedom of choice and action.

Canada was able to handle its financial affairs during the war years relatively successfully, and her record of economic stability in the post-war years compares favourably with that of most other countries. In fact, many comments on Canadian affairs that arise from sources outside Canada are extremely complimentary. Certainly real production has grown; capital investment has been large and sustained; national savings have financed a very high proportion of the resource development programme. Also Canada has enjoyed a high degree of political stability.

The business point of view on fiscal policy is that the major objective to be sought is the maintenance and extension in the domestic economy of relative stability at a high level of employment consistent with an adequate defence programme. Implicit in this objective are:

(a) Continuation of a pay-as-you-go tax policy, with tax revenues sufficient to balance needed expenditures but not calculated to produce more than a nominal surplus.

(b) A higher degree of economy in government expenditures and efficiency in government administration.

(c) A tax structure which will provide more incentive on the part of our people, both in their individual activities and in their corporate organizations, through reward for additional effort; a structure which will facilitate saving and the application of further capital investment to increase our productive capacity and efficiency.

(d) A recognition that provision for a sizable defence establishment will likely be a continuing charge on the national production.

(e) A continued attempt by negotiation to break down world barriers to trade and to extend the area within which a freer flow of goods and services may take place.

(f) The avoidance of policies, tax or otherwise, which tend to increase unnecessarily the internal cost structure or to make it more difficult to meet competition in world markets.

(g) Emphasis on broad fiscal and monetary policies to achieve objectives, rather than on specific measures and direct controls. We have had a pay-as-you-go tax policy for some years and in addition in the post-war years we have rolled up a succession of substantial government surpluses. The results for the current year will show a much smaller surplus and the budget for 1953-54 indicates a bare balance between revenue and expenditures.

The business viewpoint in Canada has been that at the existing high level of individual and corporate taxation the anti-inflationary effect of budget surpluses was lost because of the speed with which the incidence of the taxes affects the relationship between take-home pay and the cost of living and the consequent demand for compensatory wage increases. In addition business has maintained that the existence of surpluses is not conducive to government economy.

Business has expressed itself as concerned not only with the high level of government expenditures (the current budget estimates total almost 19 per cent of the estimated Gross National Product for 1953) but also with the built-in rigidities, such as public debt interest and welfare payments, which contribute to a degree of inflexibility. Although in complete accord with our defence programme, business continues to emphasize the need for economy and efficiency in all areas of government administration.

With regard to taxes, business feels that the present tax requirements, even after the reductions announced in the last budget, are still high for a developing country. Particularly with regard to the corporate tax business feels that, even at the new levels, it is still so high that it is adversely affecting corporate saving, at a time when vast amounts of capital are required for resource and other development and for the replacement of existing plant and equipment in order to improve productive efficiency.

Reference to the breaking down of world barriers to trade and avoidance of policies, tax or otherwise, which tend unnecessarily to increase the internal cost structure is in recognition of the important place which foreign trade has always played and will continue to play in Canada's development and well-being. Despite the trend toward industrialization in recent years the export of goods and services remains equal to almost 25 per cent of our Gross National Product. This emphasis on trade is one of the more striking dissimilarities between Canada and the United States and explains why Canadians generally, and Canadian business men particularly, take such a lively interest in external economic affairs and particularly in

United States' economic affairs and commercial policy. Canada now sells more than half of her exports to the United States and buys from them about two-thirds of her imports. Changes in American policies, even though they may appear to be of a minor nature, may produce very startling effects in Canada because of the disparity in size of the two countries. Mounting trade with the United States, desirable as it is, still leaves Canada with concern for the conditions of trade with the Commonwealth and with other nations. Ability to sell in world markets and be paid, and to buy and pay for the many things Canada needs, must remain one of the cornerstones of Canadian policy and endeavour; consequently business places a continuing emphasis on a freer movement of goods and services and the objective of multilateral trade and currency convertibility.

Finally, business reiterates the desirability of achieving objectives through the use of broad fiscal and monetary policies, rather than selective controls, even though Canada today has discarded virtually all controls of a direct or selective nature.

Canada in recent years has developed a comprehensive array of social legislation. These measures have been designed to alleviate existing distress and to build social defences against the time of need. Many of them have, as well as social implications, the economic implications of bolstering consumer spending through the redistribution of current income through the tax structure.

Business approves the principle of social welfare. It makes its own contribution through employer-sponsored pension plans, through life insurance, accident and sickness coverage, holidays with pay and so on for its employees. Business is a major source of funds for the many private charitable appeals which are made in Canada, but it also recognizes that there are many areas of need that can be dealt with adequately only by the state.

In this, however, business does make two points. One has already been alluded to; the weight which transfer payments, such as family allowances and universal old age pensions, have in our government expenditures and the degree of inflexibility which they impart to these. Unfortunately it has never been possible to say: "Thus far can we go and no farther." Damage to the dynamics of the enterprise system can only be assessed after the event. Consequently business emphasizes that a careful distinction must be drawn between what is socially desirable as an ultimate aim and what can be achieved at any time without damaging the system which makes our social welfare advances possible.

The second point is that social security, as provided by the state, must not become an end in itself. Business recognizes the responsibility of the individual in a free society to exert every effort to solve his own economic problems, and deplores the growing tendency to look to government for help in every difficulty. Approval of the principle of social welfare does not mean that it is the business of the state to provide those services which fall properly within the responsibility and capacity of the individual. Canada now has a population of almost fourteen and a half million, an increase of 28 per cent since 1939. There is a need for still greater population which is based on the primary requisites of defence, production and economic wellbeing. Canada's further development will require a much larger labour force, and her increasing industrial production the development of a much larger home market.

To bring to a common denominator the business point of view on the labour situation in Canada is extremely difficult. Individual views not only vary but are usually coloured by the individual's own experience. In general, however, business subscribes to the view that over the last several years there has been a significant shortage of labour, despite the growth in the labour force; and that trade unionism has not been backward in advancing its claims at every opportunity, against an inflationary background built to order for the purpose.

Harmonious employer-employee relations go much beyond that which can be imparted to them by legislation. But legislation can exert a powerful influence, either for good or evil. On the whole Canadian labour legislation exerts an influence for good. Quasi-judicial agencies certify the bargaining representatives. Procedures require the exhaustion of certain steps in negotiation and conciliation of disputes before a legal strike can take place. Collective agreements, once signed, are binding on the employer, the bargaining agency and the employees for at least one year, with grievance procedures leading finally to settlement at arbitration.

Sound administration is necessary in order that the intent of any legislation should be effective. One difficulty in Canada has been that in some instances these quasi-judicial agencies have felt themselves exempt in some degree from normal responsibility under the law. But during the last five years or so, court decisions have progressively established the fact that unions and administering officials do nevertheless bear responsibility for their acts. Another difficulty, in the case of illegal strikes, has been that though prosecutions, when upheld, provide penalties, the prosecution itself usually serves to make employer-employee relations worse. From time to time, however, there *are* prosecutions and penalties *are* imposed. Eventually this will undoubtedly result in violations of the legislation being confined within reasonable limits.

I believe that what I have written gives a fair summation of what may be considered that illusory "business point of view." Certainly not all business men would subscribe to all of them. On the other hand, few business men would take great issue with any of them. I hope that I have not overdrawn our differences of opinion. It is very easy to dwell on differences because that is where the sharp focus is, and take for granted the wide area of general agreement which makes up the whole picture.

Canadians generally, and business in particular, have several reasons for a high degree of satisfaction: there is the general acceptance of the basic philosophy of a free competitive enterprise system as a foundation stone of our development and the eminently satisfactory results of the policies which we have pursued during the war and the post-war years. There is, too, the tremendous resource development programme which is rapidly increasing our stature among the nations, and the unmistakable potential for further development, further population increase and further weight in the scales on the side of freedom-loving people.

GENERAL RESOURCES

THE HONOURABLE ROBERT H. WINTERS is the first
Minister of Resources and Development, an office
which was created in 1950. He had previously been
Minister of Reconstruction and Supply. His portfolio now includes the direction of such federal
responsibilities as forest and water resources, wild-
life, the administration of the Northwest and
Yukon Territories, the planning and implementation of public projects and services including the
Trans-Canada highway, and others.

VIII

GENERAL RESOURCES

TWO WORLD WARS and the Korean war have taught our generation an important lesson: that the present stage our civilization has reached requires great moral and economic strength both to defend the cause of freedom against aggression and to provide opportunities for better living. The success of defending the gates of Paris in 1918, the battle of the skies over Britain in 1940, are symbolic of the moral quality that enables democracies to withstand and in the end successfully defeat wanton aggression.

Economic strength has its roots in the natural resources a country possesses and the skill and imagination with which people make use of these resources. There are some exceptions to this. For example, Britain does not possess the great variety and abundance of natural resources that some other countries do, but the British people, through their creative ingenuity as a major industrialized nation, have been able over the centuries to exchange manufactured goods and highly specialized services against foodstuffs and industrial raw materials from many nations. There are countries with vast natural resources which have hitherto lacked the capital and the managerial and technical knowledge to make effective use of the treasures they possess. By and large, countries that have been fortunate enough to possess plentiful diversified resources and have made effective use of them have made great economic strides. The outstanding example is the United States, where industrial progress has been particularly rapid and where the standard of living has become the highest in the world. Canada is now well embarked on the same course.

Canada, a country of less than fifteen million people, comprises about two-thirds of one per cent of the world's population. This comparatively small country produces more newsprint, nickel, asbestos and platinum than any other nation. Canada is second in the world output of hydro-electric power, pulp, aluminum, gold and

77

zinc, and third in the production of silver, sawn lumber, and oats. In the northland, the great areas of the Northwest Territories and the Yukon, there are still vast frontiers of natural resources which have not yet been fully explored and scarcely touched.

Canada's agriculture has made great strides in mechanization and the treatment of the soil. Owing to exceptionally good weather, over 1½ billion bushels of grain were harvested last year, the largest crop in Canadian history. Canada's output in wheat alone is equivalent to more than one half that of the United States; enough to provide bread as well as cake for almost 200 million people, on the basis of Canadian consumption standards.

As to fishing, this has become in North America almost a billion dollar industry. Canada's share is continuously increasing, comprising now about one quarter of the total. If the problems of both production and marketing can be overcome, tremendous possibilities for further growth appear to be ahead. For the world's greatest stock of fish is off the east and west coasts of North America.

The forests of Canada are one of her most important sources of wealth, providing Canadians as well as many other friendly nations with a multitude of essential products, ranging from materials for shelter against the elements to the newsprint for daily papers. The productive forest area in Canada almost equals that of the United States. This means about 34 acres of forest land to every Canadian, against just over 3 to every American. With world demand for wood products rising almost continuously, Canadians are very conscious of the need to use these resources wisely and to assure their existence in perpetuity. Therefore a great deal of effort is devoted in Canada to protecting, conserving and making the most effective use of the forest resources.

There has been one innovation that may have far-reaching effects on industry in North America, and possibly the world over. The Canadian Pulp and Paper Research Institute which is supported by the federal government building upon some twenty-five years of research, has just come up with a revolutionary development— striking improvements in the processes of making chemical pulps. These changes may be used to reduce wood consumption, in some cases as much as 50 per cent. Moreover, it will now be possible to use more completely several tree species which are in abundant supply and which have hitherto been largely wasted. This might be of great importance to the pulp and paper industry of the United States, which turned into chemical pulp last year a quantity of wood over 600 times the size of Madison Square Gardens. Here is a challenge to both American and Canadian industry to produce better and cheaper commodities, while at the same time preserving for future generations one of their most precious heritages, the forest resources.

Canada abounds with lakes and rivers. We are constantly pushing back our northern frontiers, using water to turn the wheels of industry and to light the cities. Canadians now use almost twice as much electric power *per capita* as Americans do at about half the cost per kilowatt hour. So far only about one quarter of our total available water power has been developed so there is considerable room for further expansion. Two outstanding examples of undeveloped power sites in Canada are the Yukon drainage basin area in the Yukon Territory and northern British Columbia and the Hamilton River system in Labrador. The power potential of these two developments alone is estimated conservatively at over 8 million horsepower. This can be brought into perspective by comparing with it the Grand Coulee power plant, the world's largest, which has a capacity of some 2½ million horsepower. In Canada there is a known potential of about 52 million horsepower still waiting to be harnessed.

In the midst of this abundance there is still a shortage of developed power, particularly in industrial Ontario. This is one of the reasons why Canadians deem it so necessary to go ahead with the development of the St. Lawrence, which will yield over 2½ million horsepower for use by the State of New York and the provinces of Ontario and Quebec.

The atomic age and the arrival of the jet engine brought new challenges to the Canadian mining industries. Canadians responded to these challenges by pressing ahead vigorously in their search for minerals, both new and old. And as their search yielded rich finds, extensive development followed. The most remarkable feature of this development is the broad front on which progress is being made. Canadians are considerably expanding the output not only in such traditional fields as those of non-ferrous metals, nickel, copper, lead and zinc, but also in newer fields, including oil, iron ore, titanium, cobalt, uranium and other rare materials.

Some of these minerals were produced in Canada in earlier days, but the new developments are taking place on such a scale as to be tantamount to the creation of entirely new industries. And further, more and more of these metals are being processed at home. In fact, the availability of low cost power resources in many parts of our country has made it possible for Canada to engage in the processing of ores obtained from other countries. The outstanding example is the Canadian primary aluminum industry, which depends entirely on the import of bauxite as its major raw material. Canada's aluminum production is at present about half as great as that of the United States. When the new giant aluminum development at Kitimat in British Columbia is fully completed, it could and might bring the total annual production above current United States' output. Or to put it differently: Canadian aluminum production might reach a record annual output equivalent to the aluminum requirements for about one quarter of a million fighter planes. It is sincerely hoped that most of Canada's aluminum output will continue to be devoted to peaceful purposes.

Three other major developments have occurred in the mining field. Many will remember the excitement that gripped the United States following the discovery of vast oil fields and their early development in Texas. This is now taking place in Canada. Tremendous new opportunities have opened up with the finding of large reserves of crude oil and natural gas in the Province of Alberta, and the prospect is that these fields extend far beyond the boundaries so far proven. In 1946 Canada supplied only about 10 per cent of her domestic requirements from domestic production. Today she is supplying about one-third of a much larger total.

There are good prospects that within a few years Canadians will be producing sufficient oil to meet all home demands. This does not mean that Canadians expect to become self-sufficient, but rather to achieve an overall balance by exchanging regional surpluses against imports from other countries, particularly from the United States.

After a lapse of many years, great things are now stirring in iron ore mining. Two of the major developments are the further expansion of the Steep Rock mines in Northwestern Ontario and the opening up of the tremendous ore deposits in the Quebec-Labrador area. A virtually new industry is being created in Canada. In 1946 Canada produced only about one and a half millions tons. When Steep Rock and Quebec-Labrador are in full production she may be producing as much as thirty million tons of iron ore a year and vast ore bodies are still being discovered.

The atomic age has brought to the fore the pressing need for uranium. Canada is fortunate enough to have made some of the major finds in the world of high grade uranium ores. The largest discoveries have been made in northwestern Saskatchewan and the Northwest Territories, where uranium ore is now mined. But the encouraging thing is that a number of new deposits are being unearthed in various other parts of the country. Proven world deposits and production of uranium are shrouded in secrecy, but we have some reason to believe that the present expansion programme under way may make Canada the world's second largest producer in a year or two.

Plentiful supplies of uranium have facilitated the development of Canada's atomic energy research programme. Canadians have concentrated largely on basic scientific investigations and their application to man's "pursuit of happiness" in the belief that while in this generation atomic energy could be mankind's worst enemy, it could also become its greatest friend. They are working intensively to become friends with the "atom", to have it help them to work towards a better and fuller life and to aid them in the incessant fight against two universal enemies, dreaded diseases and rapid depletion of natural resources.

Canadian scientists have made such satisfactory progress towards the development of atomic power for ultimate commercial uses and in other applications of atomic energy that the Canadian Government has just recently set up an agency, Atomic Energy of Canada Limited, whose major task it is to push forward, in cooperation with private industry, its programme of making practical use of the discoveries made thus far and anticipated in the future. In fact, scientific progress has been so rapid in Canada in recent years that the time for commencing industrial use of atomic energy has been brought much nearer than many would have considered feasible only two years ago.

In the field of medicine, one of the most remarkable uses of radio-active materials developed in Canada has been the so-called cobalt "bomb." In a sense, then, it might be said that Canada too shares in the atomic bomb business. These cobalt bombs, which are therapeutical units used against deep-seated cancer, are still in the experimental stage, but we have already had a number of cautious but encouraging reports from physicians and hospitals that are using them at present. One of the first of these cobalt bombs, which are at present produced only in Canada, went to a hospital in New York. Another unit has gone to the experimental station at Oak Ridge. Two additional units are expected to be installed shortly in Chicago and Minneapolis, and orders for four or five more bombs have been accepted from different American cities. Another unit will be going as a gift to the United Kingdom by the summer. Canada is working all out on the production of these cobalt bombs to meet the many requests from hospitals at home and from a number of countries abroad.

As in other countries, radioactive materials are used as a most powerful new tool on the very frontiers of research, in biology, metallurgy and other fields. For example, Canadian scientists are now studying, in ways never before possible, how trees get their nourishment and convert it into woody tissue. From this they hope to learn how to make trees grow faster and show greater resistance to their natural enemies, insects and disease. Such studies may also lead to an increase in the productiveness of the trees, which would mean more fibres and chemicals, on which the progress of modern civilization depends so heavily.

The rapid progress Canadians have been making in developing their natural resources on a broad front has significantly changed their ways of life. Their processing and manufacturing industries have expanded greatly, covering the whole range of basic and advanced industries, all the way from steel mills to jet engine manufacture. Canadians now enjoy a standard of living higher than at any time in their history. They have also more time to enjoy the fruits of their efforts.

The development of Canadian resources is of special interest to the United States for two reasons. First, Canadian resources complement American resources in several important ways. Their forest wealth enables them to be the United States' biggest supplier of newsprint. Their mineral wealth makes it possible for them to supply the United States with important quantities of base metals and in the not-too-distant future with large amounts of iron ore. Canada's pitchblende deposits are a vital source of uranium for the United States' atomic energy programme. Canadians in turn import large quantities of industrial raw materials from the United States such as coal, cotton and oil.

Secondly, American capital and American managers, engineers and other technicians are participating in Canadian natural resources development. Even though Canadians are financing the bulk of their resources and industrial development from their own savings —about 85 per cent of the total—they welcome American participation. It hastens Canadian development and shares the benefit of advanced technology in which the United States is the world's leading nation.

Americans in turn are participating in Canadian resources development for good business reasons. They secure a dependable source of important raw material supplies near at hand. The investment, if it is wisely made, is likely to bring many-fold returns in terms of dividend payments and capital appreciation, the latter particularly attractive to some investors, for there is no capital gains tax in Canada. No wonder then that Americans like investing in Canada. Over one-fifth of United States' private investments is in Canada and a similar portion of dividends from abroad received by Americans comes from Canada.

It must be remembered that the tremendous resources that are available on the North American continent and that are being used increasingly entail both privileges and responsibilities.

The privileges comprise the opportunity of using natural resources for the good of the country and of the individuals who make the system of free enterprise work. The fact that the standard of living on the North American continent is the highest in the world and that in many fields advances in technology are unmatched abroad is perhaps some evidence that Americans and Canadians *are* making good use of two of their greatest assets, natural resources and the resourcefulness of their people.

Responsibilities entail three considerations.

First, resources are not inexhaustible. Some are renewable, like forests, but others are not renewable, like mineral wealth. Unless waste is reduced, conservation practised, and new development encouraged, Canada's heritage is being misused. Anyone who has seen thousands of acres of forest go up in smoke, communities hard hit by rampaging waters, and dust storms playing havoc with fertile fields, will understand this. Increasing attention is being paid to this problem and encouraging results have already been achieved in both the United States and Canada.

Secondly, using resources solely for war would simply hasten the end of civilization. Under present conditions using resources solely for peacetime pursuits would invite war. There is need for a balanced use of resources. Canadians must work for a fuller and happier life and be prepared and equipped to defend it when challenged. The very fact of being prepared and equipped may be the strongest deterrent against aggression. The United Nations' action in Korea, the building of a unified defence command by the Atlantic nations in Europe, and preparedness at home are ample signs that this important principle is now an integral part of the military and economic policies of freedom-loving nations.

Thirdly, to use Canada's resources solely for the national benefit would mean being deliberately blind to the hunger, misery and distress that exist in many countries. There can be no secure foundation for peace if nations who have an abundance of resources are unwilling to help their less fortunate neighbours to help themselves. Again, in this respect great strides have been made within the framework of the United Nations and its specialized agencies, through regional arrangements such as the Commonwealth Assistance Programme for Under-developed Countries, commonly known as the Colombo Plan, and through contributions by individual countries. The encouraging progress that has been made in reducing trade barriers since the end of the war is also spreading more widely the benefits of North America's wealth.

The nations of the free world have a great abundance of resources, sufficient indeed to support, with wise use, much higher living standards than many peoples are enjoying today. A vital factor in the wise use of resources is international cooperation, not only cooperation between governments on questions of trade, economic development and defence, but also cooperation between business concerns and citizens of different countries in specific enterprises, each contributing what he can best offer to the common

GRAIN TANKER ON THE GREAT LAKES

The importance of the St. Lawrence Seaway has been recognized
by Canadians throughout the last century. The grain crops of
the western prairies move to market by that route.

TRAWLER FISHING ON THE GREAT BANK OF NEWFOUNDLAND

The fishermen of Canada are the most colourful and courageous primary producers still left on this North American continent, a gallant, independent breed with pride in their heritage and in their calling.

objective. The alternative to making the most effective use of natural resources through international cooperation may well be defending our own way of life on our own shores.

FISHERIES

Mr. Ralph P. Bell is President of National Sea Products Limited, Halifax, Nova Scotia. During the war Mr. Bell was associated with the Canadian Government as Director of Aircraft Production and later as Aircraft Controller. He was also a member of the Canadian Section of the Joint War Production Committee.

IX

FISHERIES

THE FAMOUS AUTHORESS, Rachel Carson, would probably introduce the subject of Canada's fisheries with a phrase something like this: "Fish from the Sea Around Us". What a domain! From tiny periwinkle to succulent scallop and aristocratic lobster, from smallest smelt to giant swordfish, from humble cod-fish to the gourmet's lemon sole, staple of the negro in the cane fields of the West Indies, choice of the epicure in fashionable cafés!

To cover Canada's fisheries in the short space of one chapter is no easy task, for here is a great natural resource, a vocation, a sport, and an industry, or rather, several industries; a self-perpetuating natural resource of incalculable value the infinite possibilities of which are hardly scratched, a vocation over two thousand years old bathed in the mists of antiquity and steeped in romance and adventure, a sport which runs the gamut all the way from the bare-foot boy with his wattle, his can of worms and his six-inch brook trout to the multi-millionaire with his private salmon stream and his thirty-five or forty pound salmon or his private yacht and his nine hundred pound tuna. It should be added, however, that in Canada these latter are as free and accessible to the tourist, the local barber or the garage mechanic as they are to the tired business man. It is an industry of innumerable ramifications that in one of its branches alone has made more progress in the past fifty years than in the previous five hundred. Some natural resources can be reasonably accurately described statistically. Fisheries, unfortunately, is not one of them. Wheat, for example, can be spoken of in terms of acres and yields per acre. Standing timber can be described in billions of board feet and cords of pulpwood. The potential horsepower of rivers awaiting hydro-electric development can be predicted and measured with reasonable accuracy. But who can predict how many salmon, halibut, cod or haddock will spawn this year and how many will survive to reach maturity six or eight years hence? Who can say what will be the vagaries of a species of wild life with millions of miles of ocean in which to roam? The change of habitat of the lowly herring spelled ruin for one of the most prosperous communities of Europe in the fourteenth century. But that is another story. As a vocation fisheries can be spoken of statistically.

In Canada, we have 85,000 fishermen, and 20,000 persons engaged in plants on shore. Of these, two-thirds of the fishermen or 56,000 and eighty per cent of those employed in plants (16,000) work on our Atlantic seaboard. Though these figures seem small it must be remembered that Canada is a country with a population not quite 15,000,000; less than one-tenth that of the United States.

To leave our fishermen in your minds merely as a statistical reference would be a grave injustice to the most colourful and courageous primary producers still left on this North American continent, a gallant, independent breed with pride in their heritage and in their calling. This refers particularly to the fishermen of the North Atlantic. Resourceful, intrepid, adventurous, staking their all, including their lives, against the elements, all they ask is good weather, good luck and a reasonable price. Here is rugged individualism and our much vaunted free enterprise at its best.

In the field of sport, British Columbia, Quebec, Nova Scotia, New Brunswick and Newfoundland offer some of the best opportunities in the world for salmon fishing, whilst Nova Scotia is recognized the world over as the swordfish and tuna fishermen's paradise, attracting as it does annually scores of sports fishermen from all over the world. On Canada's best salmon streams, when conditions are most favourable, a kill of four to six fish a day for a skilled fisherman is not considered extraordinary, while six and seven hundred pound tuna are an everyday occurrence for devotees of that exciting sport. The record long held by the late Thomas Howell of Chicago, off Liverpool, Nova Scotia, was nine hundred and fifty-six pounds. That was broken last year when Commander Hodgson of Montreal boated one in St. Anne's Bay, Cape Breton, weighing nine hundred and seventy-seven pounds. So much for the lure of rod and line.

Now what about research? Apart from the very modest work

done by various units in the industry itself or by provincial govern-ments, the chief work in this field is carried on by what is known as the Fisheries Research Board, a body appointed and financed by the federal government, comprising scientists, civil servants and representatives of the industry. This organization maintains research laboratories, plants and experimental craft on both coasts. We Americans—we in Canada regard ourselves as Americans also—are so accustomed to the term "greatest in the world" that anything less than that seems small. The province of British Columbia, which covers the entire Pacific coast of Canada, has one river, the Fraser, which is perhaps the greatest single salmon river in the world, although the entire Canadian pack of salmon is only about one-third that of the United States, and only about sixty per cent of that of pre-war Japan.

The halibut fishery on the West Coast is under the voluntary joint administration of Canada and the United States, a control which Japan has recently agreed to recognize. The regulations are such that the United States and Canada each have an equal chance to get approximately half the annual catch.

The third fishery of substantial value on the Pacific Coast is herring.

The total annual marketed value of *all* fisheries products at the processors' level from Canada's Pacific Coast is slightly over $85,000,000.

Our inland fisheries, lake and river, only account for a marketed value of some $20,000,000 a year. Even so, they are the largest inland fresh water fishery in the world.

The Maritime Provinces, Nova Scotia, New Brunswick and Prince Edward Island, share with the State of Maine the greatest known lobster resources in the world, and these have now been still further augmented as a result of Newfoundland's inclusion in Canada.

Off the Atlantic coast between Nova Scotia and Newfoundland, there lie the largest known fishing banks in the world. A bank, in fishing parlance, is a plateau of ocean bottom 25 to 100 fathoms below the surface, a fathom being six feet.

True, Canada does not "own" these banks in the commonly accepted sense of the word, but since they lie within twelve to forty-eight hours "steaming" time from our ports, we are able to land fish from them at our plants in a superbly fresh condition. This is an overwhelming advantage with a highly perishable product such as fish, where each successive twenty-four hours between time of capture and processing means progressively rapid deterioration. Just how much of the area of these banks would lie within Canadian jurisdiction if we followed the course of Norway and Iceland and invoked what is known as the "headland to headland principle" for determining national sovereignty is not something that needs to be considered in this discussion, for Canada is one of the promoters of and participants in the International Commission for the North-west Atlantic Fisheries, which includes in its membership the United States, Canada, Denmark, Iceland, Italy, Spain, Portugal, France, and Norway, and the United Kingdom and Northern Ireland, and which recognizes the potential danger of over-fishing and is already moving to conserve and regulate this tremendously valuable natural resource. Small wonder then that here off the Atlantic coast we find Canada's most valuable fishery, the one that has been least intensively exploited to date, and the one with probably the greatest potential future. The present total marketed value of our Atlantic fishery products is "pushing" $100,000,000 a year.

Thus the total annual market value of Canada's fisheries is something in the order of $200,000,000 a year.

A moment ago it was stated that one branch of this complex industry has made more progress in the past fifty years than in the previous five hundred. In another, in spite of all the inventive genius of mankind and the myriad changes that have taken place in the twenty centuries of development since the dawn of the Christian era, it still employs the same basic methods commonly in use in the days when Christ fed the multitude with the loaves and fishes. Small wonder that it is a topic of enthralling interest. Five hundred years takes us back to the days of the Hanseatic League which flourished from the thirteenth to the eighteenth century. The Hansa, as it was called, was the world's first great international business organization. In those days the three great commodities of world trade were codfish, herring and tallow, and among the earliest privileges sought by the founding members of that ambitious undertaking was the right of fishing. It has been said that a large part of the fortunes of the League was built up on a foundation of herring. However much or little truth there may be in that statement, it is a well established historical fact that the decline in the prosperity of the Hansa dated from about 1425 when the herrings left the Baltic. Of still greater importance to us on the Atlantic coast of Canada is the fact that ante-dating even Cabot, 1497, the earliest known activities of the Scandinavians and Europeans on this coast were in the prosecution of the fisheries. At least one of the surviving firms in Nova Scotia today can trace its origin to adventurous merchants from the Channel Islands, while in the famous old fishing port of Lunenburg there is a firm in the salt fish business one hundred and sixty-four years old, still owned and operated by a direct male descendant of the original founders.

Fifty years ago the largest fish plant on the Atlantic coast of Canada comprised a few wharves and wooden buildings, a score or so of hand carts, a weighing scale or two, and some modest flake equipment. The total capital investment probably did not exceed $20,000 to $30,000. Today, a modern fish plant of substantial size and balanced proportions, in the fresh, frozen and smoked branch of the industry, may cost anything from a million dollars up. At today's costs, you can figure roughly $40,000 for every million pounds of landings to be handled. The investment per employee will run anywhere from $5,000 to $6,000, depending on the type of equipment used. A fishing vessel, at the turn of the century, cost something in the neighbourhood of $5,000 to $8,000— certainly $10,000 would have been the limit. Today, a modern diesel trawler, with all its equipment, will cost from $300,000 to $500,000. A trawler will land anywhere from three and a half to five million pounds of fish annually. The cost of a trawler will therefore run around $75,000 per million pounds of catch per year, or an investment of $15,000 to $20,000 for each member of the crew, Captain included. Even the fifty foot long liner, owned by the individual fisherman, today costs $20,000 to $40,000. It is a long cry from the dory, a hundred dollars, and the pair of rubber boots of a half century ago. To put it all in a single package, a modern plant, together with the necessary trawlers to supply the bulk of its requirements, today requires an investment of approximately $100,000 for every million pounds of fish landed annually—and this does not include the necessary working capital.

The transformation that has taken place can be traced largely to seven things.

1. The change from sail to power, and the development of the trawler, the dragger, and the power operated long liner, the three most modern methods of capture for deep sea fish that have yet been devised.

2. The development of the by-products, medicinal cod liver oil, glue and most important of all, fish meal.

3. The origin and development of the fillet, from which has developed the consumer package—the product ready for the pan—thus eliminating the time and disagreeable work formerly required to prepare it for cooking.

4. The invention and practical application of rapid freezing to fish, thus putting the product in a form acceptable to the housewife, and suitable for handling by the giant chains and supermarkets.

5. Rapid refrigerated transportation service, by rail and truck, the latter rapidly supplanting the former in the transportation of frozen sea foods. Today, fish even flies to market—and thousands of miles from the rolling Atlantic, "Airborne Fillets" are featured regularly in many a smart restaurant where fastidious customers are willing to pay a premium for delicious seafood at its best.

6. The introduction of the low temperature display case in retail outlets and the adoption of fish as a regular item of sale by the larger chain stores, and finally,

7. The almost universal use of mechanical refrigerators and so-called deep freezers in the average American homes.

The story of the development of this great industry from the primitive to the modern, interspersed as it has been with failures in the long process of trial and error, is a business romance of imagination, courage, perseverance and skill. But what of the future? The prosperity of Canada's fishing industry on the Atlantic Coast depends in no small measure on the continuation of access to the markets of the United States on terms no less favourable than those at present enjoyed. The United States has within its power, by tariff or quota action, to bring distress, and even calamity, to the entire Canadian fishing population on the Atlantic Coast, but it is unlikely that the United States will take such action. Why? Because the demand in the United States for the products of this fishery has far outstripped the capacity of its own East Coast fishing industry and there seems to be no reasonable likelihood of further expansion in the production of this industry in the United States. The United States has a population of well over 150,000,000. Canada's population is approximately 15,000,000. Last year Canada's purchases from the United States totalled $2,977,000,000. The United States purchases from Canada were $2,307,000,000, and only $88,000,000, or 3.8 per cent of that, were products of Canada's fisheries. Canada, with only 15,000,000 people bought from the United States $670,000,000 more than the United States bought from Canada, and paid cash. There is no question of economic aid here, no debts that ultimately have to be written off and shouldered by the long-suffering and hard-pressed United States taxpayer. Here is an old reliable cash customer who pays on the barrel head in good United States dollars, and who for every man, woman and child in Canada, spent $200 last year with the United States while for every man, woman and child in the United States, Americans spent last year in Canada less than $16.

As an illustration of one small aspect of this trade and some of the problems that from time to time confront us, two of the chief products of Atlantic fish are frozen groundfish, and ocean perch fillets. The consumption of these commodities in the United States has doubled in the past twelve years. In very round figures it is today something like 200,000,000 pounds a year. Production in the United States has not kept pace with this increase, and for some years Canada has supplied practically all the difference, having been the supplier in steadily increasing quantities since there first developed a gap between United States' production and the market demand. Within the past three or four years in particular, foreign countries such as Iceland, Norway, Denmark, Greenland, England, the Netherlands, France and West Germany, with no historic participation in the United States' market in fish, finding themselves with surpluses in the varieties referred to, have diverted these into the United States market, largely on consignment, without regard to the capacity of the market to absorb these shipments. The result is that an oversupply has developed, with a temporary demoraliza-

95

tion of the market to the detriment of United States and Canadian industry alike. As a result, a campaign for quotas and higher tariffs is developing in the United States. In the past two years production of this commodity in the United States has averaged approximately 110,000,000 pounds, leaving 90,000,000 pounds to be supplied by imports. During the same period Canada's sales of these items to the United States averaged 48,000,000 pounds, or, roughly, half the spread. As a matter of fact, millions of pounds of the frozen fillets Canada ships to the United States are for their own producing and processing companies in their own packages and in their own wrappers all ready for the retail trade. This 48,000,000 pounds represents less than one-third of a pound per capita of the population of the United States, whose total consumption of fish is slightly over eleven pounds per person per year. This means that the product under discussion represents but three per cent of the total annual fish consumption in the United States.

Canada is by all odds the United States' best customer, and it is simple, practical business common sense to keep a good customer satisfied. Canada is not trying to sell something that would compete with production in the United States. Quite the contrary! It is something required to fill the gap between the United States' productive capacity and the market demand. The fact that some outsiders have come in and temporarily upset the market is not something for which Canada should suffer through restrictions which might possibly be imposed. Instead of telling the European countries that their salvation lies in breaking down their trade restrictions and tariff barriers, Americans and Canadians should practise what they preach at home. Nowhere could it be more natural. Nowhere would it have better hope of success. Such an example might easily electrify and inspire the democratic world.

AGRICULTURE

Mr. John G. Diefenbaker is Member of Parliament for Prince Albert, Saskatchewan. He was first elected to the House of Commons in 1940 as a member of the Progressive Conservative Party. In April, 1945, he was an adviser to the Progressive Conservative Delegation to the United Nations Conference at San Francisco and in 1952 was a member of the Canadian Delegation to the United Nations, New York.

X

AGRICULTURE

CANADA HAS THE THIRD largest land area in the world next to Soviet Russia and Communist China, but only sixteen per cent of that area is suitable for agriculture. While the developments in Canada's mineral industry have captured the imagination, the mineral production last year being $1,275,000,000, yet the total farm income far exceeded in value the income from mineral production. Farm income was $2,787,800,000 which, because of lower farm prices, was $38,000,000 below the high of 1951. In 1952 the Gross National Product was eight per cent over 1951 and one of the main reasons for that increase was the heavy yield of the wheat crop. The Canadian prairies (with only 1/169th of the world's population) last year produced the fourth largest crop of wheat in the world, a crop worth $949,000,000 or 45 per cent of the value of the entire Canadian field crop production. Canada's annual production of wheat will feed 100 million people.

There are 700,000 farms in Canada and the total investment in agriculture is little less than that of all manufacturing industries. Forty-two per cent of Canadians lived on the farms less than fifty years ago. Today there are only twenty-two per cent. Canadian farmers find themselves in the same paradoxical position as all American farmers. They realize that the world needs food, but they are fearful of producing because of the danger of surpluses. They realize that the world population is twelve per cent greater than it was in 1939 and that food production is only nine per cent greater. The Canadian farmer can see dangers ahead. He is prosperous today, but he realizes that whereas last year farm production increased in Canada by twelve per cent, farm income in fact decreased and the cost of the things that the farmer must purchase increased by approximately five per cent. The Canadian Federation of Agriculture announced recently, "While Canada today is undoubtedly enjoying an era of extraordinary prosperity, agricultural producers particularly in the field of livestock and livestock products find themselves victims of an economic squeeze between declining farm returns and rising farm costs."

For several generations, Canada will produce more wheat than can be consumed. At present the amount on hand is 700 million bushels, compared to carryovers of 405 millions in 1952 and 242 millions in 1951. Part of this 700 million bushels will be disposed of in the months ahead.

In its point of view, Canada is a nation of free enterprise, but that does not apply to agriculture in so far as wheat is concerned. Now with a crop of a billion dollars in value, the marketing is done by the state under a Federal government Wheat Board. There have been criticisms of the operation of the Wheat Board on the grounds that it entered into bulk sale agreements with Britain, that it is today a member of the International Wheat Agreement, and that, being a member of both these bulk sale agreement organizations, prices have been lower than they otherwise would be. It is, however, only fair to say that the Canadian farmer as a whole believes in bulk sale agreements designed to provide security of market and freedom from fluctuations in prices, fluctuations which are sometimes unnecessary, and caused by the pressure of external events.

Surpluses of other farm products are being accumulated—seventy-six million pounds of canned pork, considerable quantities of dairy products and others. The deteriorating dairy situation is in part due to the effects of the necessary embargo by the United States to prevent the spread of foot-and-mouth disease, but it is intensified by the restrictions imposed by the United States in August of 1951 on the imports of fats, oils and dairy products. About this measure the Canadian government in a message to the State Department on February 11th, 1953 expressed "its serious concern at (the) infringement of international agreements" brought about by the import restrictions. The United States embargo to prevent the spread of hoof-and-mouth disease has resulted in the loss to Canada during the last year of a market for 370,000 head of beef cattle, ninety million pounds of dressed beef and 50,000 head of dairy cows.

Canada has just completed negotiations in Washington for a two-year extension of the International Wheat Agreement which ends July 31st, 1953. Canadian farmers demanded an increase in the existing maximum and minimum prices ($1.80 and $1.20) coupled

LAYING THE INTERPROVINCIAL PIPELINE

This 1100 mile pipeline was built to carry oil into the bigger markets of the East. From the head of the Lakes the oil is taken by oil tankers to Sarnia refineries in Ontario.

THE ALCAN PROJECT, KEMANO, BRITISH COLUMBIA

The availability of low cost power resources in many parts of our
country has made it possible for Canada to engage in the processing
of ores obtained from other countries. The outstanding example is
the Canadian primary aluminum industry.

with an escalator provision to assure increased prices, should costs of farm production continue to rise. During the course of the present agreement Canada's wheat—of a superior variety—has been sold at forty cents less per bushel than the world market price.

For several years following a wheat agreement with Britain, many hundreds of millions of bushels of wheat were sold at prices which ultimately turned out to be some seventy cents per bushel less than could have been procured on the world market. Widespread complaints ensued, and in 1951 Parliament contributed sixty-five million dollars for Western wheat farmers to make up in part for this loss.

Markets for farm produce other than wheat have suffered the loss of the British market. Cheese exports to Britain that amounted to 200 million pounds in 1904 are now almost non-existent. The bacon and ham exports which amounted to 150 million pounds a year and reached a high level of 700 million pounds a year during the last war, have diminished to a trickle. Among reasons given for this are the increase in farm production in Britain and the devaluation of currencies, which weakens the possibility of Canadian farm products competing with those from overseas countries. In consequence Britain is obtaining her food needs under long-term agreements at lower prices, such as the fifteen-year agreement with Australia to take over that country's exportable surplus of beef and lamb; a five-year contract for butter and cheese with New Zealand and an agreement for dairy products with Denmark and other countries.

As Canada's population increases the home market will use much of the dairy production. The only other market for Canadian farm products (other than wheat) is the United States and for this market, so long as trade channels are kept open, it has an advantage in beef and dairy cattle.

What will be the future of Canadian agriculture?

1. Production will continue to rise and, where there is full production, surpluses of products in general will be built up, and in particular, for several generations there will be hundreds of millions of bushels of wheat each year for sale on the world market.

2. The home market will absorb a greater share of the propor-

tion of farm products other than wheat, providing there is general prosperity.

3. To provide fair prices and security against depressed prices, floor prices in line with costs of production will have to be maintained.

4. Surpluses of farm produce will have to be disposed of by extending the industrial and chemurgic uses.

5. National projects in greater measure must be undertaken to preserve lands from erosion and to remove marginal lands from production.

6. Finally, Canada's international markets for farm products must be extended.

Canada's mineral production will play a tremendous part in building the industrial machine of defence in the United States. Agricultural products, too, will play an important part, for if Communism marches, agricultural production among NATO countries other than Canada and the United States, will be materially reduced if not altogether destroyed. Canada's productive machine for agricultural products must be maintained at high levels in order to meet the possibility of war, yet at this very time Canada's international trade in farm products (other than wheat) is almost exhausted. It is the opinion of this writer that now, more than at any time in history, the people of the United States are favourably inclined towards removing unnecessary barriers against the import of Canadian farm products and allowing such importation.

The tariff acts of the early and late 'twenties in the United States may have been justified as a national policy then, but no longer are such expedients justifiable when weighed in the scales of international danger. The United States requires Canadian raw materials of mine, forest and oil-well in order to build effective defences. The closing of United States markets to Canada's agricultural products will deny to Canada the maximum preservation of an agricultural economy which should be encouraged to grow and expand. Canadian agricultural production will not only raise the standard of living of both Canada and the United States; it will enable each to fulfil the human demands of hungry stomachs of those everywhere who stand against Communism and who cannot stand unless they are strong in body and in material defences. Farm markets in the United States for Canadian farm products will go far to enable Canada to maintain its agricultural productive plant in these twilight days of peace, and at the same time, assure that should the curse of war again be brought upon us, Canada's agricultural production will be one of the most effective elements in an all-out and full mobilization for survival.

INDUSTRIAL PROGRESS

Mr. James S. Duncan is Chairman of the Board and President of Massey-Harris Company Limited. During the early part of World War II Mr. Duncan was asked to organize the British Commonwealth Air Training Plan and was made Deputy Minister of National Defence for Air. He later returned to Massey-Harris to direct the Company. He has served on many important bodies and has been Chairman of the Combined Agricultural and Food Committee, Washington, and of the Dollar-Sterling Trade Board.

XI

INDUSTRIAL PROGRESS

It is now nearly half a century since Sir Wilfrid Laurier forthrightly said to his fellow countrymen, "The twentieth century belongs to Canada." Laurier's high-sounding phrase must have provoked smiles at that time in Washington and in London, and to some, at least, of Laurier's five million fellow citizens, it must have sounded like the catch phrase of a political leader, rather than the deliberate expression of a statesman's vision.

Moreover, there were times during the past half century when many Canadians found themselves recalling Laurier's phrase with a certain sense of embarrassment, so clear did it seem to some of them that the momentum of Canada's development had been arrested.

And yet, despite the violent stoppage of immigration, which occurred in August, 1914; despite the severe burden of World War I, (which the people of Canada bore so courageously and with such determination from the first day to the last); despite the setback Canada suffered because of railway bankruptcy following upon the years of conflict; despite all these things, there was a more rapid rate of growth of population and production in Canada during the first quarter of the twentieth century than anywhere else in the British Dominions, or even in the United States of America.

This was before the stock market madness of the late nineteen-twenties, before the breadlines began to be manned, and before World War II loomed up as a sand-storm looms up over a shelterless desert.

Because of these disturbances, which affected all North Americans alike, Canada's progress during the second quarter of the twentieth century was less impressive than during the first, and it seemed as though there were less fervour and less enthusiasm than during the first part of the century. And yet, for those of strong faith and vision it was evident that this was but a period of pause, a prelude, a gathering of strength before the resumption of the upward climb.

It was in the year 1935, that Canada, fighting her way upward from the depths of the great depression, stood upon the threshold of the period of her greatest development.

There are many reasons why Canada, with a population of but fifteen million, in a world of two billion, four hundred million, is the third exporter of the world; why her standard of living is the highest after that of the United States; why Canada has balanced her budget with a large surplus for seven years in succession; why her export trade has jumped from $738 million in 1935 to $4 billion 400 million in 1952, a sixfold increase in seventeen years; why the national debt has been reduced by no less than 17 per cent since the end of World War II; why the Canadian dollar is free and at a premium even over the United States dollar. But two reasons are paramount. The first is the treasure-trove of her natural resources, the abundance of her agriculture, the wealth of her subsoil, the vastness of her timberlands; the second, the character of her people, descendants predominantly from two great European races, each having carried down from its forefathers characteristics and traditions, which, notwithstanding superficial differences, have been felicitously blended into an harmonious whole.

It is this asset of character, born of tradition and of a simple, hard-working agricultural background, and of that closeness to the soil, which is characteristic of Canada today, which expresses itself in Canada's political stability and economic realism. It is upon these two great pillars that rest not only her past achievements, but also her hopes and ambitions for the future.

Canada's progress has been impressive in many fields. I should like in this chapter, to refer more particularly to her industrialization and the mainsprings of its progress.

During the first half century following Confederation, agriculture remained the main source of Canada's income and employment. Two wars, a greatly increased rate of accumulation of domestic capital, the inflow of foreign investments, always welcome and increasingly confident, the development of low cost sources of hydro-electric power, the rapid advance of managerial and technical skills have profoundly altered the pattern of Canada's economic life.

From small and simple beginnings, not very much more than

one hundred years ago, when Canada's manufacturing establishments only supplied pioneering needs for bread, for buildings materials, for implements, sleighs and wagons, and simple household furniture, there has developed a greatly diversified, highly skilled and rapidly expanding secondary industry, which now produces over $12 billion worth of manufactured products per annum.

The first main impetus to industrialization came with World War I. Military demands were directly responsible for creating new refining capacities for non-ferrous metals, and for the expansion of Canada's small steel industry, and the development of many secondary industries.

The second period of extensive industrial expansion occurred in Canada between 1926 and 1929. This was a period of particularly rapid growth in Canada's pulp and paper industry, in the manufacture of transportation equipment, especially in the automotive field, and in the output of non-metallic minerals and chemical products.

The long years of depression which followed were not without their gains for Canada. Under the pressure of intense competition, manufacturing enterprises streamlined their organizations, improved their designs and manufacturing processes, and prepared themselves to meet all comers, at home or abroad.

The third period of industrial growth commenced with the outbreak of World War II in the autumn of 1939. Canadian manufacturing industries, though by then considerably expanded, were unprepared for the avalanche of military orders. Yet conversion to a full war footing was accomplished in the short space of between eighteen months to two years. Expansion of capacity was particularly striking in such sectors as toolmaking, and the manufacture of electrical apparatus, precision instruments, chemicals, synthetic rubber, aluminum, aircraft, military vehicles, and a great variety of munitions of war. New factories were built and shipyards constructed.

At the height of the industrial war effort in 1943, it has been estimated officially that about three out of every five persons employed in Canadian manufacturing plants were working on war orders.

The fundamental contribution of World War II to Canada's industrialization was one of quality rather than quantity. The pressure of military demand for large quantities and great diversity of equipment, with rigorous inspection standards, fine limits and low tolerances, compelled industry to develop new skills and techniques, and more closely integrated processes than anything which had been previously known.

Of Canada's immense output of munitions and war equipment, about 70 per cent was made available to allied nations, mainly as Mutual Aid contributions.

It should be mentioned here that Canada, who alone among the Allies received no Lend-Lease Aid from the United States, and asked for none, was not only fortunate in being able, through Mutual Aid, to assist her Allies, whose sacrifices had been greater than hers, but carried alone and unaided her own burdens of war.

Two-thirds of the wartime industrial structure, which Canada possessed in 1945, was found readily adaptable to peacetime uses. Large capital outlays were required for reconversion, and these were forthcoming. By 1947, Canada's greatly enlarged industry was back again on a peacetime footing and ready to play its ever-growing and ever more important part in the reconstruction programme of a world torn and shattered and disorganized by war.

The year 1947 heralded in the greatest period of Canada's industrial growth, one during which in each successive year a new record of achievement was rung up. From the figures now available for 1953, it appears that this process of improvement and expansion is still continuing.

In the brief period of five years, from 1948 to 1952 inclusive, new investments in Canada have totalled more than $20 billion. This represents more than 20 per cent of the Gross National Product of Canada during the same five years.

What then are the causes of this amazing industrial growth in a country of less than fifteen million people, which was predominantly agricultural until thirty-five years ago?

Canada's industrial expansion has, undoubtedly, been twice shaped by war and the period of replenishment of the empty shelves which followed it has been and is now accelerated by the rearmament programmes both at home and abroad. But one must look deeper for the underlying causes of Canada's sustained surge of growth in its steel mills, power plants, metal and oil refineries, extractive industries and fabricating plants. These are to be found in the physical environment and political climate of Canada itself, and in the character of her people.

Let us review, without placing these in order of importance, some of the sources from which Canada's economic and industrial strength has found its origin. There is the abundance of raw materials, the basis of all industry, which has given such a sustained impetus to Canada's development.

There is the agricultural wealth, which was the origin of prosperity, and which continues to play a dominant role in the nation's economy.

Important, also, is the fact that capital from abroad has always been welcomed, has never been restricted and has been left free to come and go as it pleased.

Canadian development in the early days would have been very slow if, like many other countries today, Canada had refused to allow foreign capital to come in and help to develop natural resources, agriculture and industry, or if, having let it come in, had placed restrictions upon it, which would have discouraged future movement of funds in the country.

In some respects, Canada is no longer dependent on borrowing from abroad for the development of her natural resources; in fact, this year about as much of Canadian capital will go abroad as came in.

Then too, there has been the awakening of our people to the necessity of developing our export trade over a widely diversified group of countries throughout the world. For too long, Canada has relied on the easy solution of selling over 80 per cent of all exports to two friendly nations speaking her own language, to the United States and the United Kingdom. Post-war experience and the decline in purchasing power of traditional British markets have made Canada realize that if she is to be a successful exporter, she must go out into the highways and byways of the world and merchandise her product. She must take advantage of this ferment, this leaven, which is working in the great masses of the people in so many of the free countries in the world today, of that striving towards a more abundant life and a higher standard of living, so evident today, which is carrying with it larger national income and greater purchasing power for goods produced both locally and abroad. That Canada has been reasonably successful in spreading exports over a wider area can best be illustrated by the volume of exports to South America, where our exports have increased from $18 million per annum in 1937 to $275 million in 1952.

Another factor is the rapid growth of Canada's population, which increased by more than 150 per cent during the first half of this century, and has recently been growing at a steady rate of approximately 3 per cent per annum; and the great strides which have been made in the consuming power of the nation, which can best be illustrated by the average annual income, which, at present day prices, increased from $700 *per capita* in 1929 to $1,100 in 1952, and the high and sustained rate of domestic investment.

Equally important with the material aspect already referred to has been the political stability and freedom from excessive governmental interference and regulation. It is of more than passing interest that throughout the 85 years of history since Confederation, regardless of the government in power, there has been a consistent attempt to encourage the enterprising, the venturesome and the thrifty, and to keep restrictions and barriers to trade and business intercourse to a minimum. Exceptions were made in times of war, when controls became obligatory, but these were relaxed and ultimately discontinued, just as soon as the reasons for their imposition were no longer present.

Any recital of the factors which have given impetus to Canada's economy and particularly to her industry, would be incomplete if we did not mention the great advantages which have been derived from her proximity to the United States, not only because of access to United States' markets, but also because of the stimulation of their dynamic economy.

Canada, too, is facing up to one of the main requisites for increased world trade in a realistic manner, as is evidenced by her changed policies in regard to the progressive removal of trade barriers. Whereas from 1879 to 1939, Canada consistently maintained a national policy of tariff protection, there has been a distinct movement away from that policy in recent years. Canada has been an active participant in all post-war international conferences aiming at the overall reduction of tariffs, and a wholehearted supporter of any movement which would tend towards the gradual freeing of world trade. She recognizes that trade, to flourish, to develop, and particularly to be permanent, must be on a two-way basis, and that if Canadians are to sell a lot abroad, they must also buy a lot from abroad.

Canada's performance is not attributable solely to the wealth of her natural resources. The human element in a nation, in a business or industry, or in any other walk of life, is always the predominant factor. It is more important than bricks and mortar, more paramount than wealth, more transcendent than boundless resources.

Canada's natural resources will not be selfishly used. In two World Wars, and in the years of uneasy peace which have followed, she has given abundant proof that she is ever to be found on the side of an orderly world, of a liberal attitude towards trade, of friendliness and goodwill towards her fellow men.

Canada is moving steadily toward the liberal concept of a world where trade barriers will be lessened, and where she will prosper, not by the selfish handling of her own abundant resources, but by the growing living standards and prosperity of other nations.

The wealth of her subsoil will be at the service of others; it will assist the free world in assuring not only continued industrial progress, but security in this atomic age.

SCIENTIFIC ACHIEVEMENTS

DR. G. EDWARD HALL is President and Vice-Chancellor of the University of Western Ontario, where he was previously Dean of Medicine. During the war he was in charge of Aviation Medicine for the R.C.A.F. He has been Director and President of the National Cancer Institute and Chairman of the Committee on Medical Education of the Canadian Medical Association. Dr. Hall is a member of the National Research Council and a Fellow of the Royal Society of Canada.

XII

SCIENTIFIC ACHIEVEMENTS

IN GIVING A PICTURE of science and research in Canada, the background has to be Canada itself, a young giant sprawling over an area of 3,845,000 square miles, smaller in size only than Russia and China, with a mainland and island sea coast of nearly 60,000 miles, with some 250,000 square miles of fresh water area, with an inland navigable waterways system driving 2,338 miles from the Atlantic ocean into the heart of the country. The destiny of Canada is shaped, in part at least, by its great neighbour, whose land unfenced except for a few gate posts extends across 4,000 miles of Canada's southern fields and another 1500 miles between its Pacific and Arctic coasts. More than half of the total land area used to be listed officially as waste and other land, rock, muskeg and tundra. But that was before Canada's reawakening. The background of our picture begins to reveal form in some detail. We see in a Canada extending over 48 degrees of latitude and 88 degrees of longitude, part of it tucked wholly, or in part, south of more than one-half of the states in the United States, and embedded in the north under the frozen cap of the Pole, a thriving, healthy, but sparsely populated young Dominion, possessing one of the world's great stores of natural resources.

People must appear in the picture at this stage. The great natural resources of land, of waterfalls, of forests and rocks, are resources which are recognized as assets today, but were regarded as barriers by our forebears. They became assets of more than just personal importance only when Canadians learned how to use them, and by using them intelligently Canada has become a "nation on the march." But the Falls of Niagara, the immensity of the waters of the Great Lakes, the formidable rocks and muskegs of the pre-Cambrian Shield, the lurking darkness of the forests of the north, the spacious land of the west, could still be barriers if it had not been for the adventurous spirit of people, the men and women who with vision, with purpose and with profit in mind, conquered these barriers and turned them into assets. No-one can regard the mines, forests, lands and waters as other than great assets and great resources, assets and resources, though, which God alone has given to Canada, given in trust to be used intelligently and in modesty in the interests of the Canadian people now and in the future.

A few details should be added to that picture. In spite of the fact that Canada is undergoing a strengthened industrial development and that over the last forty years there has been a radical shifting in the distribution of population from rural to urban areas, it should be remembered that agricultural production has actually increased 22 per cent even since 1939. Some concern has been expressed, even by expert economists, that the decline in the rural populations in the food producing nations of the world would result in insufficient food for the growing populations. But perhaps these people forgot about science. There is no question that the shift to urban communities is real. In 1911 considerably more than half of Canada's total population lived on the farms. By 1951, with double the 1911 population, 60 per cent of the people lived in urban centres, and the shift is still continuing. Remember that in 1911 there were less than four million people in rural areas in Canada and that forty years later there were five and a half million people living in the same rural areas. This fact is important, particularly when we consider the greatly increased production of farm products. Back in 1921, as a great agricultural country, the gross value of production of primary agricultural products in Canada was just under one and a half billion dollars, but with the increased industrialization of Canada since that time, what has happened? These values in 1951 reached three billions. If secondary agricultural industries are added to this value of primary agriculture, more billions of dollars are added, providing a livelihood for hundreds and thousands more Canadians and giving stability and balance to the rapidly increasing industrialization of the country.

It is difficult for people to realize that only fifty years ago the total mineral production of Canada was sixty-five millions of dollars; sixty-five million in 1901, doubled by 1915, redoubled by 1928, doubled again by 1940, and doubled again by 1951 to more than a thousand million dollars. Nickel, copper, lead, zinc, aluminum, are the non-ferrous metals which are so vital to industry and to a national economy. If the coal of Alberta and Nova Scotia, the iron which is being located in so many areas, and her fabulous stores of base metals do not place Canada as a modern industrial nation, then the continued success in discovering ever increasing areas of crude petroleum and natural gas in western Canada certainly shall. A country now of fourteen and a half million people, scattered over half a continent, Canada last year had a Gross National Product of goods and services of twenty-three billions of dollars. Science and the will to progress had made this possible.

It is quite natural for science to develop or to be applied along those lines which will most benefit the country in which the scientist works. This, just as obviously, is not the case in pure fundamental science or in basic medical research, where the inherent interest of the scientist dictates the direction and scope of his own research. Simply, therefore, for the sake of understanding and not for categorization, three broad, but necessarily overlapping, areas of research will be recognized in this chapter. At the one extreme is the so-called fundamental or pure research, where science is solely concerned with the understanding of natural phenomena, the search for truth, and the establishment or enunciation of principles. Purely arbitrarily, the second area of research will be called applied research, where the scientific worker in the solution of specific problems uses basic knowledge, facts and techniques and applies them in the ultimate solution of his particular problem. The third area of research may, again purely arbitrarily, be classed as developmental research, or engineering or applied science. Perhaps besides these three areas of research, there is yet another field of scientific activity (whether it may be called research is a matter of opinion). the very important field of surveys. Scientific background, research experience and sound scientific discrimination are the essential qualifications of those engaged in this work. It can be said, therefore, that there are four areas of scientific activity in the natural, physical and biological sciences: fundamental research, applied research, engineering development and scientific surveys. These areas are certainly not well defined. Indeed in the study of so many problems, they are hopelessly confused. The scientist does not, nor should he, in general, try to classify his scientific activities into compartments, let alone even to recognize that such exist.

How, then, are scientific or research activities organized in Canada? Unconsciously perhaps, research, other than fundamental research, is the reflection in general of the relative significance of the values of commodity production, and it could hardly be otherwise. In Canada primary agriculture, industry, mines, and lands and forests, in that order, receive the greatest attention from research and on them, in the same order, are made the greatest research expenditures; with one exception, atomic energy. In this fascinating field it is important to realize that Canada, the great producer of uranium, since the war has been expending its research energies towards the utilization of atomic energy, fission products, and radioactive isotopes, for a peace time economy. The cobalt sixty cancer units, the first in the world, developed in Canada and used in Canada, are providing more adequate treatment for those suffering from the devastating disease of cancer. This is just one of hundreds of new uses of atomic energy in Canada. The future uses are incalculable. Not to mention Canada's achievements in medical research, with its insulin, its ACTH etc., would be to overlook a most significant feature of her total research programme. Some three million dollars will be spent this year, outside of university funds, chiefly in the support of medical research in the universities of Canada in fundamental and applied research throughout the medical science departments. On a *per capita* basis that type of expenditure is a worthy effort.

Research in Canada, as in the United States, is carried out under four main auspices: universities, government research laboratories, research foundations and industry. Organized research on a national basis started in 1916 with the establishment of the National Research Council of Canada, which since that time has played a very vital role in Canada's wartime and peacetime research. Radar, which Canada gave as a useful tool to the world, is just one example of this work. The National Research Council has its own major research laboratories in Ottawa, a Prairie regional laboratory in Saskatchewan, and a Maritime regional laboratory at Halifax. The work carried on within these laboratories is chiefly applied research and directed towards the solution of major industrial problems, or through a combination of pure and applied research, directed towards the utilization of Canada's natural resources and the creation of new industries for the manufacture of the newly

developed products. The National Research Council is also responsible for a very significant programme of scholarships and grants in
aid of research in the natural, physical and medical science fields,
the greatest part of the money being granted to highly qualified
members of the universities of Canada for the support again of
fundamental research.

In general, the National Research Council of Canada carries on
work comparable to the National Research Council, the Bureau of
Standards and the Academy of Science in the United States. As in
the United States too, several of the Canadian federal departments
are engaged in various phases of scientific activity such as Agriculture
with its extensive experimental farm service and its very effective
science service, Mines and Technical Surveys with their energetic
and extremely valuable surveys and service divisions which
have meant so much in the development of Canada's vast
natural resources. Although there are other branches of the federal
government such as Defence where research and other scientific
activities are features of their work, those mentioned are sufficient
to indicate the major role of government in research activities. At
the provincial level, too, comparable but less extensive research
foundations or research councils are active in special fields, particularly those immediately concerned with the development of the
resources within the respective provinces, with the stimulating of
the utilization of waste products and with helping to develop new
products and new industries. Group research in Canada is in its
infancy as compared to the maturity of industrial association
research in Great Britain. Each of the cotton industry, the woolen
industry, the coal industry, the iron and steel industry, and dozens
of others, has its own group research supported by the members
of the industry for the benefit of the whole industry. In Canada
the Canadian Pulp and Paper Association is showing the way to
other groups. For example, some of the steel companies in Ontario,
supporting collectively the development of a sponge iron in association with the Research Council of Ontario and the Ontario Research
Foundation, have solved a major problem of scrap iron supply and
created a new industry within the industry. The future of group
research in Canada could well be significant. Relatively few
industries in Canada have their own research and development
laboratories. Some do and their laboratories have paid handsome

returns. Many other companies are associated with major organizations in the United States and the United Kingdom where the research is carried on. This in most cases is a mistake, not only from the point of view of creativeness, application and product development, but also from the consumer and public relations aspect. The people of a progressive country should not be denied by big industry the right to participate in the research, the development, the utilization and production of products made from the resources of that country and sold and used by the people of that country. Canada has the resources and the raw materials. It produces the scientists and should have a realistic share of the industrial research laboratories, where young Canadians knowing Canada, loving Canada, thinking Canada, looking to the future in Canada, could use their scientific abilities in Canadian industry and in the other laboratories.

The universities of Canada are, as are the universities in every free country, the chief centres of fundamental research. Although this type of research is carried out to some extent in government laboratories, departments, and in research foundations, the universities are the traditional home of fundamental research activities. It is through general adherence to this philosophy that undergraduate and graduate teaching and research are combined in the same departments, from which comes a steady stream of well-trained, enthusiastic, young and highly qualified men and women to take their places in Canadian educational institutions, in Canadian industry and in the many Canadian scientific activities, as integral parts of Canadian assets and Canadian resources.

But what is research? The basis of research is obviously knowledge, but research is something in addition. It is an attitude, an attitude of curiosity. It is a state of mind, discerning, discriminating, judicious, patient, inspired. It is a mood, a mood possessed by people, and that is why there is no clearcut definition, why no precise lines of demarcation are warranted. For instance, a young mathematical physicist is interested in the kinetics of molecular discharges in gaseous media; what is the rate of movement of electrons across an area of nitrogen, of hydrogen, or of argon? What is their path, their energy dissipation? That is certainly a fundamental study. Facts are accumulated, reports written and placed in the libraries of the world. Principles have been established.

On the other hand, a better understanding of the nature, forces and effects of the fascinating and awesome aurora borealis, the Northern Lights, is of vital significance to any country lying in the northern hemisphere, where air transportation, navigation, and radar control are important. The fundamental study of the kinetics of molecular discharges takes on new significance and the problem becomes one of applied research in the field of astrophysics. With this new interest of a national kind, the work could be accelerated. Modifications might well be effected, through engineering development, in navigation and in radar equipment, but the one and the same physicist has been a key figure throughout.

A biologist is interested in the principles of larval development, the effects of water temperature, adhesion to rocks, the mechanical effects of freezing, the oxygen tension of the water; in effect the study of the life cycle of the black fly, the ecology and physiology of a minute biting insect. Surely this is again a fundamental study in biology; but the gold of the Yellowknife, the clicking geiger counters of the northwest, the radar outposts, and the new farms fingering along the valleys of the countless rivers beyond the wheat lands, have brought people to those black fly areas, building homes and living in new lands, and hundreds of cattle have died in a single valley because they could not cope with that little black insect which emerges from the water covered rocks of moving streams. The problem of the black fly is no longer just a nuisance problem to bushmen and ardent fishermen, but a problem of economic importance to Canada. Those same biologists planned what might also be called a classical experiment in applied research, mathematically calculating the rate of flow of a winding swollen river over a distance of many miles, the concentration of chemical required to be effective against the larvae two inches below the water's surface, yet not to harm other biological life, the diluting effects of distance, currents, eddies and falls, the absorption of the chemical by organic matter in the river, aircraft speed, wind currents and their effect on the chemical to be sprayed from the aircraft. All of these calculated with precision based on scientific wisdom and the fundamental knowledge of the black fly larvae assured the perfect results which followed. Every calculation of this planned experiment was correct within ten per cent, as determined in the actual applied research, and the black fly was eliminated in a one hundred mile area. Frontiers of the north are being pushed back by science.

Here is yet another type of research, called scientific survey. It is interdependent on the other phases of research. Twenty-five years ago Norfolk County bordering on the north shore of Lake Erie in southwestern Ontario was essentially an unproductive area of abandoned farms and blow sands with sparse areas of fertile top soil protected by struggling strips of reforestation. Today that same county is one of the most affluent in Canada all because of the efforts of a soil chemist. He took thousands of samples from thousands of test spots, did as many thousands of chemical analyses, used techniques and methods evolved by fundamental science and laboriously plotted by grid and profile the results of his work. Such results could have been filed away in scientific journals and the work acclaimed by his colleagues. But this scientist, and he is a scientist, was interested in soils and land utilization too. In searching the literature or recalling the results of soil surveys in other countries he became aware of the similarity of the chemistry of the Norfolk soils with that of the best tobacco lands of Virginia. More than 85,000 acres of flue-cured or Virginia type tobacco and another 11,000 acres of burley tobacco were grown in 1953 in those Lake Erie counties and in Canada a total production of 140 million pounds of tobacco was harvested at a farm value of more than 55 millions of dollars last year. It is a strange coincidence that in this same Norfolk County by yet another type of modern survey, aerial survey, and the use of the magnetometer, extensive iron ore deposits have been located, proven by drill to be in the pre-Cambrian rocks lying like a shim under thousands of feet of pleistocene in which were accidentally found rich deposits of gypsum. This once poor county, rich now in its tobacco, fruit, bean and corn lands, may soon be a strange mixture of greenhouses and slag dumps, of orchards and endless bucket conveyors, of tobacco barns, harbour facilities and wall-board factories. The farmer, the scientist and the engineer have combined to help make Canada great. Of the scientific surveys none can have meant more to any country than the Geographical, Geological and Geodetic Surveys. The history of geology in Canada is essentially the history of the development of Canada and its natural resources. Perhaps no country in the world has given so much scientific attention to research in aerial photography and the associated techniques as Canada. Stands of forests are now cruised from the air; scientific instruments and unique contrast photography are locating undreamed of bodies of ores. The surface of our pre-Cambrian Shield has only been scratched. The developments in aerial photography and surveys are shattering the armour of the north while other aerial technical advances are guiding the fishing fleets to record catches in the reaches of the North Atlantic. Science obviously knows no barriers. Since the establishment of the Surveys in 1842, more than 30 per cent of the total area of Canada has been surveyed, and after the publication of their reports, by canoe, by dog-sled, by air and on foot go the prospectors, and the gold, silver, nickel, coal, iron, the oil and the gas, the magnesium and uranium are found; the landing strips and the roads, the docks and the rails and the homes and the factories are only a short way behind.

These things are science. These things too are research. These are the things which are developing Canada. These things help to make Canada a nation. On the basis of Gross National Product, our total expenditure on research through the tax dollar equals that of the United States, but to develop a frontier country of vast area, of difficult terrain and of unlimited opportunity, our expenditures of both the tax and the private dollar for research and development must of necessity go still higher. Progress in research now is production in the years ahead. Canadians are proud of their scientific achievements as they are proud of their past. They accept the assurances of scientific developments to come as they accept the future of the country itself and if they recognize the potentials of their country, the God-given resources at their disposal, and their own character and strength, then through hard work, intelligence, continuing modesty and scientific achievements they can make their dreams come true and make Canada a country of destiny. In this scientific and atomic age, surrounded by plenty, they have a real concern for the recognition and preservation of human values.

PETROLEUM DEVELOPMENT

MR. NATHAN E. TANNER is President of Merrill Petroleums Limited, Calgary. He was previously a member of the Alberta Legislature. He became Speaker and later, Minister of Lands and Mines. With the development of the natural resources of Alberta, the Department of Lands and Mines was divided and became the Department of Lands and Forests and the Department of Mines and Minerals. Mr. Tanner was named as Minister of both Departments and held these portfolios until he resigned to take over the Presidency of Merrill Petroleums Limited in 1952.

XIII

PETROLEUM DEVELOPMENT

O IL, TOGETHER WITH NATURAL GAS, is one of the most important industrial commodities in Canada, the United States, and in the whole world. All the wheels of industry turn on oil. All petrochemical industries are dependent on oil and gas, and much of the world's fuel and power is derived from oil. Industrial development and consequently living standards are closely related to oil, and it is becoming more and more important every day in Canada's security. In fact, oil and gas development in Western Canada has probably done more than any other single thing to spark the general glow of activity being felt in every phase of life in that part of the country.

At the outset I should like to deal briefly with one unique difference between the ownership of minerals in Canada and in the United States. In the United States most of the minerals are owned by the person who owns the surface rights on the land. In Canada, however, where oil development is being carried on, the minerals are mostly owned by the Dominion or the Provincial Government and are referred to as "Crown" property. Prior to 1887 the mineral rights were included in the title to the land, but from that time on, when title was granted to a homesteader or to any other resident obtaining title to the land, the minerals were reserved to the Crown. The result is that from 60 per cent to 90 per cent of the minerals in the Prairie Provinces are owned by the Crown and approximately 100 per cent in the North West Territories. Most of the balance is owned by the Hudson's Bay Company, the Canadian Pacific Railway and the Calgary and Edmonton Corporation, and some by individual landowners. This has had many far-reaching effects on the development programme. It has greatly facilitated the carrying out of an orderly development with a good conservation programme, as the government has had full and unquestioned authority over its own minerals. It makes it possible for the oil company to deal with only one or two owners or landlords, while in the United States it may be necessary to deal with many owners in order to get a suitable land play. It makes the rentals and royalties payable to the Crown, and, therefore, the public treasury has profited. This means that the benefit is enjoyed by the people as a whole, through the government treasury, and not, as in the United States, by the relatively few landowners who happen to be fortunate enough to own the minerals under the surface which they bought.

Though the Provinces of Alberta and Saskatchewan were formed in 1905, and Manitoba in 1870, the natural resources, including the mineral rights, were retained and administered by the Dominion Government until 1930. The whole of the North West Territories is still administered by the Dominion Government. The Government of British Columbia has had full control of its resources since it became a Province in 1871.

Though the area in which oil is found in Western Canada is administered by five different authorities, the policies governing development are more or less similar. As government policies and regulations play such an influential part in the development of any country, the most important should be considered. The Alberta system, under which most of the development has been carried on, may be taken as a sample.

The oil and gas rights owned by the Province are administered by the Department of Mines and Minerals. They cannot be sold, but may be acquired under lease by filing on a block of acreage, or through the medium of a Petroleum and Natural Gas Reservation or a Natural Gas Licence. Only the Petroleum and Natural Gas Reservation will be dealt with here. A reservation, which is essentially a prospecting licence, may be obtained on an area not exceeding 100,000 acres, and a maximum of two such reservations may be held by an applicant at any one time. The purpose of the reservation is to allow time and exclusive opportunity for all forms of exploration, including exploratory drilling, to be carried on. For the privilege of holding such a reservation the holder must carry out an active exploration programme, satisfactory to the Government, and report regularly the progress made. A reservation may be held for a maximum of three years, providing the holder complies fully with the regulations. Current regulations require that the applicant for a reservation pay a fee of $250 and deposit with the Government $2500 for each 20,000 acres, as a guarantee that an active exploration programme will be carried out. Without going into detail as to all the requirements, the regulations provide that if the holder of the reservation has complied with these provisions, including the exploration programme, he may lease any time before the expiration of the permit 50 per cent of the reservation in blocks of not more than nine sections. None of these blocks may be adjoining but must be separated by a corridor of one mile or may form a checkerboard pattern. The lease is held for a period of twenty years and is renewable as long as it is productive. The lessee pays a rental of $1.00 per acre and a graduated royalty ranging from 5 per cent to 16⅔ per cent, according to daily production, on the oil produced. The areas not taken under lease become Crown Reserves and are disposed of by the Crown on a competitive basis as and when the Crown sees fit. Sales are held at intervals, where those who are interested can bid by sealed tender a cash bonus for the right to lease the land. The successful bidder is granted a regular lease, on which he pays the rental and royalty as set out above.

The sale of Crown Reserves has proved to be a lucrative source of revenue to the Province. Up to the end of 1952 it had sold the right to lease 1215 quarter sections of Crown Reserves for over $93,000,000, with one quarter selling as high as $3,110,000. This bonus revenue, together with the royalties and rentals collected by the Government during the last six years, has amounted to over $178,000,000, approximately $55,000,000 of which was collected during last year. At the same time industry has felt secure in its position and has carried on a very active programme with most encouraging results.

Another factor that has contributed greatly to the confidence with which the American, British and Canadian investor has participated with his risk capital in this rapidly growing industry, is the orderly manner in which the development has been carried on. Much of this is due to the conservation programme under the direction of the Petroleum and Natural Gas Conservation Board. This Board was set up in Alberta by an act of the Legislature, and was given full authority pertaining to the drilling for, and production of oil. Boards are also being established in the other provinces to regulate development.

Canada is in the most fortunate position of being able to profit from the experiences of the United States. The conservation programme in the 1930's in some of the oil states there had progressed very materially before crude oil was encountered in Western Canada, and as a result Canada was able to accept and build on the programmes then established, and was able to apply the principles of conservation while new fields were being opened up.

Under this programme the Conservation Board has full authority to make regulations for the purpose of determining that drilling and all other operations for the production of oil and gas be carried on according to the best known engineering practices, and of giving each lessee or owner the opportunity of obtaining his just and equitable share of the production of any pool.

The Board endeavours to prevent waste and to secure the optimum recovery of oil or gas from the reservoirs by fixing the maximum permissive rates of production in accordance with sound engineering and economic principles. The maximum permissive rate governs production as long as there is a market for all of the oil which can be produced legally. When more oil can be produced legally than the market demands, production is regulated by the Board which fixes the provincial allowable and then allocates to each field or pool its fair share. The allocation of each pool is then divided among the producers in the field or pool. This is proration to market demand. The main purpose of proration to market demand is to enable each producer to obtain his just and equitable share of the production from any pool and to enable all producers to share in the market. Those in the industry have full confidence in the Petroleum and Natural Gas Conservation Board and realize that everyone is going to receive fair and equitable treatment.

The part of Western Canada in which oil is most likely to be found is the area which includes the sedimentary basin. More particularly it is that part shown on Figure 1 and which, as you will see, extends from the Rocky Mountains on the west to the pre-Cambrian Shield on the east, a distance of 800 miles; and from the U.S. boundary on the south to the Arctic Ocean on the north, a distance of 1800 miles. This is where most of the development has taken and will continue to take place. This basin covers an area of over 800,000 square miles, which is greater than the total

Department of Resources and Development

RESEARCH IN FOREST PRODUCTS

It may not be too fanciful to suggest that with the new products
and by-products now in prospect, the pulp and paper industry may
one day become a chemical industry, with the result that we will
make a much fuller and more diversified use of our forest resources
than we have ever done in the past.

MINING AT STEEP ROCK

After a lapse of many years, great things are now stirring in iron ore mining. Two of the major developments are the further expansion of the Steep Rock mines in Northwestern Ontario and the opening up of the tremendous ore deposits in the Quebec-Labrador area. A virtually new industry is being created in Canada.

area of Texas, Louisiana, Oklahoma, Kansas and California. Though this whole basin will not be productive, oil is being found scattered throughout the area.

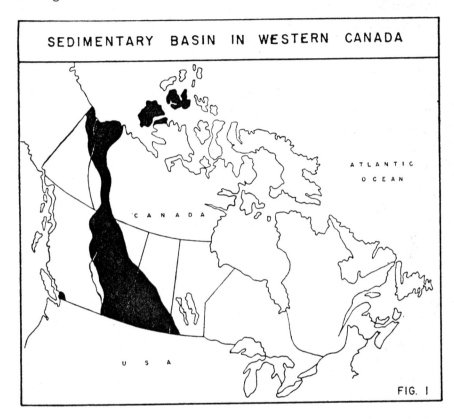

SEDIMENTARY BASIN IN WESTERN CANADA

FIG. 1

It is true that the extent of the oil development and the production in Canada is very small in comparison to that of the United States, and to some, at first glance, might even seem insignificant. On the other hand, it must be realized that practically all of the development has taken place in the last six years. At the beginning of 1947, when the Leduc strike was made, Canada had reached a low ebb in the search for and production of oil; in fact, serious consideration was being given to the possibilities of making synthetic oil from natural gas. Some $23,000,000 had been spent with little or no avail. Besides this Canada was producing less than 10 per cent of her petroleum requirements, or just barely enough for the Province of Alberta. Today her possible production would meet over 50 per cent of all her requirements. In 1947 the total proven reserves of crude oil were sufficient only to meet Canada's requirements for less than one year. Today, just six years later, these reserves have been increased by more than twenty times. In other words, they are sufficient to meet Canada's requirements for more than ten years, in spite of the fact that the nation's consumption has more than doubled.

Though figures are always more or less monotonous, and often boring, I know of no other way of showing comparisons and of actually measuring the progress which has taken place; therefore, I shall use what I think are most significant figures and I hope interesting. In doing this I am making use of figures and charts, some of which have been prepared and used by others at different times, and here I wish to express my apologies and appreciation to them. The figures to which I refer are as follows:

WESTERN CANADA
Progress: 1946 to 1952

	1946	1948	1950	1951	1952
Exploration and Development Expenditures—Millions of Dollars	12	50	165	230	300
Land being explored Millions of acres at year-end	20	55	131	168	214
Geophysical parties Maximum number during year	11	62	125	155	189
Exploratory Wells drilled in year	119	155	309	345	840
Producing Oil Wells 1. Drilled during year	64	250	834	814	1236
2. Producing at year-end	490	703	1936	2712	3650
Production Thousands of barrels daily—Potential	20	40	168	205	300
—Actual	20	34	80	133	173
Reserves at Year-end Millions of barrels	72	500	1100	1376	1679
Miles of Trunk Crude Oil Pipelines Operating	31	31	63	1242	1600
Under Construction	—	12	1179	400	750

One of the best ways to measure the confidence that those engaged in the oil industry have in the future of Canada is to look at the amount of capital that they are prepared to risk in exploration.

Compare the figures for the years 1946, 1951 and 1952. They show that in spite of the fact that such phenomenal development had taken place up till 1951, an accelerated rate of development was experienced in 1952. In fact, 1952 was a record year in every phase of the industry. From the figures given it will be seen that the money spent in exploration increased from $12,000,000 in

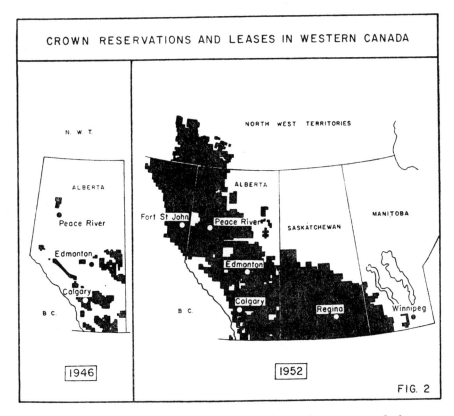

CROWN RESERVATIONS AND LEASES IN WESTERN CANADA

1946

1952

FIG. 2

1946 to $230,000,000, or about twenty times, by 1951, and then to $300,000,000 in 1952. This is money spent in the search for oil and development and does not include the large amount of capital expended for refineries, pipelines, etc.

As you will note from the figures before you, the money spent in the search for oil has had very encouraging results. The area of land being explored increased from 20 million acres in 1946, to 168 million in 1951, and 214 million in 1952, or over ten times the amount. A comparison of the number of geophysical parties in the field will give some idea of the work being done on the land held. In 1946 there were eleven, in 1951, 155, and in 1952, 189, or seventeen times the number. Also, during that same time the number of exploratory wells jumped from 119, in 1946, to 345 in 1951, and 840 in 1952. These are wildcat wells drilled in unproductive territory. The number of producing wells increased from 64 to 814 to 1,236, i.e., 50 per cent more producing wells were drilled in 1952 than in

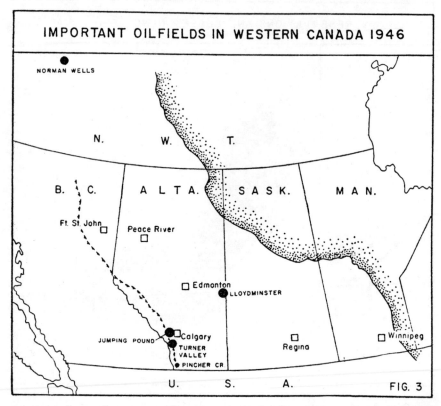

IMPORTANT OILFIELDS IN WESTERN CANADA 1946

FIG. 3

1951, and nearly twenty times as many as in 1946, with the result that there were 3650 producing wells at the end of 1952.

Another impressive figure is the potential daily production of 300,000 barrels as compared to 205,000 in 1951, and 20,000 in 1946. The established reserves have increased from 72,000,000 in 1946 to 1,376,000,000 in 1951, or nineteen times as much, while today the reserves have been increased to 1,800,000,000 barrels, or by more than 400,000,000 barrels.

In order to carry this oil to market, 1600 miles of pipeline have been built, 750 are under construction, and another 625 committed, which will make a total of nearly 2000 miles. More will be said about pipelines later.

Figures 2, 3 and 4 give a better idea of the activity that has taken place. Figure 2 shows the Crown reservations and leases in Western Canada for 1946 and 1952; Figure 3 shows the number of important or significant oil fields in Western Canada in 1946 as

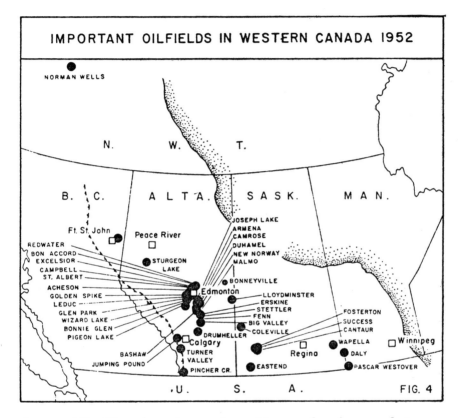

four, while Figure 4 shows that this number increased to 40 during 1952. Since that time other fields have been discovered and these fields are scattered throughout the whole of the sedimentary basin and extend from Norman Wells in the North West Territories to Manitoba, being a distance of over 1500 miles, in which production has been found.

Another very interesting and most encouraging feature of the oil and gas industry in Western Canada is the large reserves of natural gas that have been established during the past few years. During 1951 they were increased from 4.7 trillion to 6.8 trillion, or nearly 50 per cent, and in 1952 they were increased another 50 per cent to over 10 trillion. In fact, gas has been found in ever increasing quantities and in new areas throughout the producing area. However, due to lack of markets for the gas, hundreds of wells have been capped and condensate fields (wet gas fields) have been closed in and will remain closed until a market is available. There has been a general feeling among the industry that export would be permitted this year and the necessary markets made available in the very near future. Great hope was added to this belief when the Premier of Alberta stated recently that the finding of an export market was of urgent importance. This can only be interpreted as meaning that he is convinced that we have the reserves to justify an export market and that the gas will be made available at an early date. The closed-in condensate fields will be brought into production and drilling will continue in areas where the gas wells are capped. Money will be made available for further exploration as the gas is sold and as a result the whole programme will be speeded up. It would also make available thousands of barrels of high grade oil and other raw materials, such as propane, butane and sulphur, which are so badly needed. For example, a condensate field, if it were to produce 100,000,000 cubic feet of gas a day (which it could produce, and much more), would yield out of that wet gas 3,000 barrels of high grade oil, 700 barrels of butane, over 500 barrels of propane and 300 tons of sulphur every day, and when one thinks of those industries being closed in because of lack of markets for the gas, one can see how discouraging this would be for the investors. As the market is made available for the gas, it will have an important effect. This condition exists because the government was determined to see that the needs of the people were protected before any market was made available for the gas outside the province.

As pointed out before, in 1946 Canada was producing less than 10 per cent of her requirements, while today, though her rate of consumption has doubled, Canada is able to produce over 50 per cent of her needs. At an accelerated rate of development comparable to that which has been experienced, Canada will be producing enough oil within the next few years to meet the whole of her requirements, which at that time might well be in excess of 550,000 barrels daily.

Another way by which we may show the importance of the oil

area in Western Canada is to compare the sedimentary basin in Western Canada with the Central Basin of the United States, which includes the states from North Dakota and Montana on the north, to New Mexico and Texas on the south. In this Central Basin

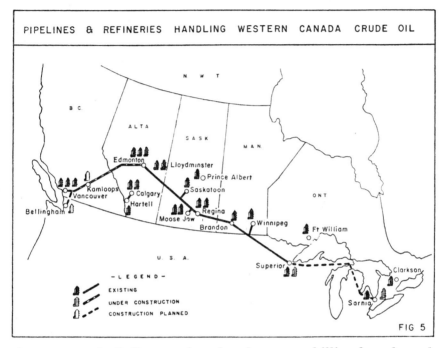

PIPELINES & REFINERIES HANDLING WESTERN CANADA CRUDE OIL

FIG 5

the amount of oil discovered to date is over 45 billion barrels, and is certainly not all that will be found. By taking this figure and adjusting it to the Canadian picture, it would not be too optimistic to conclude that the oil reserves in Canada over a period of years might well be in excess of ten times what they are today. If this proves to be true, Canada will have not only sufficient oil reserves to meet her own requirements for years to come, but will be in a position to contribute greatly to the areas deficient in oil.

Due to lack of refining and transportation facilities, Canada is producing at a rate far less than her potential; in fact, an average of only 167,000 barrels are being produced daily, while her potential production is 300,000 barrels.

As early as 1949, less than three years after the Leduc discovery, more oil was being produced than was needed to meet the Prairie requirements, and plans were made for the construction of the

Inter-Provincial pipeline from the Edmonton area to Superior, Wisconsin, at the head of the Great Lakes. Figure 5 shows this line together with the extensions. This 1100 mile pipeline was built in 1950 at a cost of $90,000,000 and carries the oil into the bigger markets of the East. From the head of the Lakes the oil is taken by oil tankers to Sarnia refineries in Ontario. This requires large storage tanks to care for the production during the winter months, when the tankers cannot operate.

In order to cope with the expansion that has taken place and is continuing to take place, the Inter-Provincial Pipeline has announced its intention to extend its pipeline from Superior to Sarnia, a distance of 625 miles, with a 30″ pipe, the largest diameter oil pipeline on the continent. This extension will cost $74,000,000 and will be completed in 1953. This will make it possible to transport oil to Sarnia from the head of the Lakes the year round, at an initial carrying capacity of 100,000 barrels daily. This, together with some looping of the present Inter-Provincial pipeline, will make a total daily market east of the Rocky Mountains of approximately 200,000 barrels. In order to increase this market it will be necessary to build in stages the greater part of another pipeline parallel to the present Inter-Provincial pipeline. Even with this market east of the Rockies being able to take 200,000 barrels daily, there is at present a surplus of approximately 100,000 barrels daily seeking a market. The next move then was to commence the building of the Transmountain Oil pipeline across the Rocky Mountains, also shown on Figure 5. Though the British Columbia refining capacity was only 40,000 barrels daily, the line was commenced with the idea of putting through an initial flow of 75,000 barrels. Now, however, in less than one year of the commencement of the line, and before it is completed, another pump is being added to the 24″ diameter pipeline now under construction, bringing the initial capacity up to 120,000 barrels daily. The ultimate daily capacity is 200,000 barrels. Though this programme to some seems over-optimistic, we are convinced that the States in the Pacific Northwest, which are now being supplied from the California oil fields, will require more and more Canadian oil as California is less and less able to supply the ever increasing demand. In fact, a new 35,000 barrel refinery is being built in Washington State, which will be using Canadian crude as early as 1954, and it is not at all unlikely that more refinery capacity will be built in that area and crude oil from Canada will be called upon to supply their needs. At present approximately 4,000 barrels of crude are going into the refinery at Wisconsin, and with crude going into the Pacific Northwestern States, Canada will be in the happy position of returning to the United States some of the crude which we have been receiving for so many years.

To supplement the great reserves of oil and natural gas, we have in Western Canada the Athabasca oil sands. These oil sand deposits are about 300 miles north and a little east of Edmonton, and possess one of the world's largest sources of petroleum and hydrocarbons. Estimates as to the probable liquid content of these huge deposits have been made by the Dominion Department of Mines and the United States Geological Survey and others, and range from 100 million to 300 million barrels. These oil sands are exposed for a distance of over fifty miles along the Athabasca River, running north from Fort McMurray, and extend for a distance of about thirty miles east and west of the river.

As a result of work done, the oil sands are found to yield about one barrel of bitumen per cubic yard of sand; the overburden varies from nothing in certain areas to several hundred feet, and drilling indicates that the sands range from very thin bands to deposits over 200 feet in thickness. The idea of mining and processing large quantities of sand to recover oil is perhaps a radical idea to oil men, but that such an operation could be conducted without difficulty has been amply demonstrated by many large strip mining operations on this continent.

For many years members of the oil industry and the Canadian and Alberta Research Councils have been experimenting to try to establish economic methods of mining the oil sands, separating the bitumen from the fine sand grains, and breaking the tar-like product down into a range of usable petroleum products.

The Government has granted to individual companies eleven reservations, comprising approximately 550,000 acres. These companies are continuing field evaluation of the oil sand deposits, method of extraction—including the *in situ* method of recovery— and research generally, in an endeavour to cut the costs and perfect a process. Altogether much progress has been made, and today only a fairly narrow margin of costs separates the oil sands from commercial development in competition with normal crude oils. In years to come that margin will almost certainly be eliminated, and the Athabasca deposits of north-eastern Alberta will play a major role in the economy of Canada.

Though 1952 proved to be a record year in every phase of the oil and gas industry, with the present active programme, with more and more land being explored, with more geophysical parties in the field, with the promise of gas export, with the building of new oil pipelines and the extending of the existing pipelines, with oil and gas now being produced in all four of the Western Provinces and with new oil fields being discovered, 1953 promises to be the brightest and most productive of all.

PULP AND PAPER

MR. ROBERT M. FOWLER is President of the Canadian Pulp and Paper Association. For some years he practised law in Toronto. On the Rowell-Sirois Commission on Dominion-Provincial Relations he acted as legal secretary to the Chairman. Later he was appointed Secretary and General Counsel of Wartime Prices and Trade Board, Ottawa. He has been President of the Canadian Pulp and Paper Association since 1945.

XIV

PULP AND PAPER

IN THE PREVIOUS CHAPTER Mr. N. E. Tanner wrote about one of the great new economic developments in Canada. I am to write about one of our older industries—old, at least in the sense that it is a well-known part of the Canadian economic picture. But there are many new things, too, that I hope to tell you about the Canadian pulp and paper industry. There has been, in the last three years, a major upsurge of activity in scientific research in this Canadian industry. It may not be too fanciful to suggest that with the new products and by-products now in prospect, the pulp and paper industry may one day become a chemical industry, with the result that we will make a much fuller and more diversified use of our forest resources than we have ever done in the past. It is over-simplifying the long-range results that may come from scientific research in the pulp and paper industry to say it may be possible that newsprint will some day become a by-product. That is probably an inaccurate picture, as newsprint should always be a major part of Canadian production; but there will be many other products and when they are developed, more efficient use will be made of the forest assets with which Canada is so richly endowed.

Canada has one of the major forest resources of the world. Her wooded area is exceeded only by the tropical forests of Brazil and the forests of Russia. Forests occupy over 1,300,000 square miles, or 60 per cent of the land area of the ten provinces. The productive forest area totals 765,000 square miles, some 10 per cent larger than that of the United States. But there is one important difference between the two; almost all of the productive forests in the United States are economically accessible, whereas Canada has over 260,000 square miles that the Dominion Forest Service now classifies as productive but economically inaccessible. In other words, this area almost the equal in size, although not in fertility, of the commercial forest area which supports the great pulp and paper industry in the

Southern States, is growing trees which cannot at present be harvested economically.

In addition, much more wood will be obtained from the forests now occupied as silviculture is improved and the serious losses from fire, insects, and disease are reduced. As much wood is consumed in Canada by these scourges each year as goes into the manufacture of pulp and paper. To date, Canada has had ample supplies of wood and there still appears to be a comfortable margin to meet growing world demands. With proper care, raw materials can be provided for a substantial additional production. But it is now clear that the Canadian forests are not inexhaustible. Fortunately the pulp and paper industry is taking a leading part in forest conservation.

In recent years there has been a major change in the world wood supply picture. In many countries demand for forest products has caught up with the rate of forest growth. European forests were seriously overcut during the war and post-war years. In the countries of Northern Europe, where they practise excellent forest conservation, wood utilization appears to be just about in balance with the forest growth. Here in this country great and successful strides are being made to increase the supply of trees, but demands for wood fibre are also growing at a great rate. Only in Canada is there such a substantial potential for increased production of pulp and paper products to meet the world's needs. And these needs are growing rapidly.

In the United States the growth has been spectacular. At the beginning of this century the average citizen of the United States consumed about 60 pounds of paper and paperboard a year; today he consumes about 390 pounds. In other countries the rates of individual usage are much lower: in Iran, 8 pounds; Japan, 23 pounds and France, 63 pounds. But as the economies of older nations recover from the effects of the war and as the underdeveloped areas progress and raise their living standards, there will be a growth in their demands for pulp and paper products which could be substantial.

It is fair to say that consumption of pulp and paper is both a good measure of modern economic development and also a prerequisite for an improvement in living standards. In the last twenty years there has been a great increase in the use of books, magazines, and newspapers; and as new human needs and wants develop, they are being met by turning to wood fibres as the raw material: paperboard containers have largely displaced wooden boxes; paper milk bottles have claimed part of the market from glass bottles; and, in a non-paper field, rayon and acetate fibres made from wood have challenged the textile markets of wool and cotton. These and many other developments have been reflected in rising *per capita* consumption.

In addition, the number of heads in the world is increasing rapidly. We can picture this increase by imagining a city of 60,000 people appearing somewhere on the map every twenty-four hours. These new people will need supplies of pulp and paper products.

Against this picture of rising population and increasing consumption *per capita*, Canada's forest reserves take on great importance. It is fortunate—for Canada and for the world—that this potential for growth exists, for pulp and paper is in many ways the basis for industrial development and a raw material of democracy.

Today the pulp and paper industry is Canada's largest industry. In the United States there is a great and growing pulp and paper industry. In absolute terms it is larger than the Canadian industry—in fact about two and a half times as large in volume of production. But in relative terms, it is less important to the American economy than the Canadian pulp and paper industry is to Canada. Among Canadian industries pulp and paper stands first in value of production, employment, total wages paid, and by a substantial amount first in capital invested. It is the largest industrial buyer of goods and services in the Dominion; it uses one-third of all the electric power generated for industry and Canada is the second-largest producer of hydro-electric power in the world. The annual value of Canada's pulp and paper output is one and one-quarter billion dollars. Its exports this year will be close to a billion dollars in value and will account for 23 per cent of all Canadian exports to all countries and about 35 per cent of exports to the United States.

There are some ninety pulp and paper companies in Canada operating 130 mills in seven of the ten provinces. Their major products in volume are newsprint and pulps. But, in addition, the mills produce fine papers, wrapping paper, tissues, paperboard and many other products made from cellulose. Between them these mills make over a thousand varieties of pulps, papers and paperboards, and specialty products.

But any such statistical summary is apt to be dull. It does not give a picture of the colour and romance of an industry such as this; nor of the scope and magnitude of the industrial skills required to provide you with your morning newspaper or the paper cups you use without thought of how they reached your hand.

The story of the industry starts deep in the northern woods, remote from any settled community. The demand for wood has pushed Canadian pulpwood operations far into the hinterland. In several instances Canadian companies are cutting beyond the height of land on watersheds draining into the Arctic Ocean. Roads have had to be built to reach these pulpwood stands; and wood is cut and hauled many miles by truck to be dumped into the headwaters of streams that flow south to the mills. There, perhaps a year and a half or two later, it moves into an enormous, highly-mechanized, mass production factory. Whatever may be the theories about bigness in industry, it is inevitable that the mills making newsprint and other papers must be big, with large high-speed machines and heavy equipment for handling the incoming wood and the bulky out-going product. From one of the more modern machines operating, as is customary, night and day for six days a week, there flows in that time a ribbon of paper 20 feet wide and 2,600 miles long. You might think of it as covering a twenty-foot highway from New York to San Francisco. And that is only one machine for one week. There are 137 newsprint machines in Canada, although not all of them, of course, are as wide or as fast as the one used as an example.

In spite of major increases in newsprint capacity since the war, it seems to be a steadily shrinking percentage of total Canadian production. Newsprint production increased by about one-third between 1946 and 1951, while the production of pulps of many kinds and qualities rose by over 60 per cent. In this period Canada became the largest exporter of pulps in the world, and in 1952 over 1,800,000 tons of pulp went to the United States. That amount represents only about 10 per cent of total United States pulp supply, but it is important to the maintenance of the high levels of pulp and paper consumption in the United States and is the sole source of supply for many important converting mills in that country. In addition, the production of fine papers, wrapping papers, paperboard, tissues and specialties has increased just over 40 per cent

THE RED BARN, PETITE RIVIERE

The most independent, the most daring, and the first to look at Canadian scenery through Canadian eyes and in a highly decorative way of their own were the members of the Group of Seven who really struck a national note and for fifteen years, from 1915-1930, ruled over the artistic world in Canada. Of these A. Y. Jackson, who painted The Red Barn, was a leading member.

PAPER FOR THE PRESSES OF THE FREE WORLD

Whatever may be the theories about bigness in industry, it is inevitable that the mills making newsprint and other papers must be big, with large high-speed machines and heavy equipment for handling the incoming wood and the bulky out-going product.

since 1946. These products are generally excluded from international trade by effective tariff barriers throughout the world, and their production has therefore grown mainly to supply expanding domestic needs. With their relatively faster growth, the production of pulps and papers other than newsprint increased from 40 per cent of our total production in 1946 to about 45 per cent in 1951, and their vigorous growth is expected to continue.

In 1952 Canadian newsprint production of almost 5,700,000 tons was 54 per cent of all the newsprint produced in the world. About 6 per cent of our production was consumed at home, about 8 per cent went to countries overseas, and the balance went to the United States, a total of over 4,800,000 tons. This Canadian supply provided about 80 per cent of all the newsprint obtained by the United States last year. Back in 1946, they obtained about the same proportion of their total supply from Canada, but received nearly 1,300,000 tons less in 1946 from Canada than they took last year. In other words the growth of Canadian newsprint capacity has largely contributed to the spectacular growth of newspapers in the United States in the last six or seven years. Canadian newsprint mills have added nearly 1,100,000 tons to their productive capacity since 1946, most of it in response to the rising demand in the United States. Incidentally, this *increase* in Canada is almost exactly the same as the entire newsprint capacity in the United States today.

Two conclusions may be drawn from the growth of Canadian newsprint capacity. The first is that it has come in response to demand. During the war there was built up an unsatisfied demand that could not be met because of wartime shortages. This pent-up demand was suddenly released when wartime controls were removed and for several years there was a shortage of newsprint, in the sense that every consumer could not buy as much extra newsprint as he wanted. But the United States producers added nearly 400,000 tons and Canadians nearly 1,100,000 tons to their capacity with the result that today the supply of newsprint has caught up with the demand. The newsprint shortage throughout the world has disappeared with all producers operating at close to their expanded capacity.

This major expansion of Canadian newsprint capacity has been accomplished by private producers who have responded in an enterprising way to the opportunities of an expanding market, without subsidies, special tax concessions, official floor prices or any other form of government intervention. If more newsprint is needed, there is no doubt that it can be provided by private initiative without the need of government promotion and assistance. This is a fact of importance in the newsprint industry. I hope we will never come to a time when the free press of the world is dependent on government assistance for its principal raw material. If it ever comes, I question if the press can long remain truly free.

From the point of view of Canada a second conclusion may be drawn. The fact is that today and for many years the United States has obtained from Canada from 75 to 80 per cent of its newsprint requirements. Canada has proved itself to be a reliable source of supply for the expanding needs of the United States. In face of these facts, it seems strange that in the last year or two there have been frequent statements by a number of United States politicians, supported by some publishers, which protest against what they call the "dependence" of the United States on a "foreign" source of supply. They have gone on to propose various government measures by way of subsidies, loans and special tax concessions, to stimulate newsprint production in the United States.

Canadians, particularly in the newsprint industry, believe in competition and do not fear competition from other mills wherever they may be built. They need only pass the test that they be economically sound and defensible as private ventures in relation to efficient manufacturing techniques and availability of markets. As proof of this attitude, companies with large interests in Canada have participated in two of the three newsprint mills recently built in the Southern States. It would appear unwise for any national government to expand a domestic industry by "forced draft", doing so for the obsolete reason that existing supplies come from "foreign" sources.

Perhaps this recent attitude among some politicians in the United States toward newsprint is a dying issue and the mere residue of an old form of economic isolationism. But Canada is concerned about it. The question of newsprint is only an example of a more general discomfort in the United States over their growing need to depend on "foreign" supplies of materials they require. If this attitude is widespread or should grow, it has some undesirable political implications; no one likes to be regarded as a "foreigner" for this is a word that seems inappropriate for neighbours and allies. It also has bad economic implications; it runs counter to the basic belief in the virtues of competition. Moreover, it ignores the point that to export you must import. Newsprint is Canada's largest export commodity to the United States. If the United States should become self-sufficient in newsprint, Canada would cease to be the largest single market in the world for American exports.

There are many examples of the growth of United States interest and curiosity about Canada in recent years. It can be seen in the spate of newspaper and magazine articles and in the flow of United States dollars and businessmen across the border to stake out a share of Canada's booming economy. Canadians welcome all of this and apparently Americans like what they have seen; they like our way of doing business, our government set-up, and the fact that Canadians believe in the same economic and political principles as they do. We venture to hope that in this process of discovering Canada, Americans will come to realize how inappropriate it is to think of this country as a "foreign" source of supply.

CANADA'S MARKETS

Mr. E. J. Umphrey is Vice-President and Director of Sales of General Motors of Canada Limited, Oshawa. He served the Company in Winnipeg, Regina and Calgary and was assistant manager for western Canada. He was zone manager for the Province of Alberta and later for the Province of Quebec. He became Director of Sales in 1942.

XV

CANADA'S MARKETS

BOTH AS A CANADIAN and as a salesman, I welcome the opportunity to give my views, sketchy and generalized as they may be, on the subject of Canada's markets. Other and more qualified people have written about Canada's historical development, its government and its relationships with business. They have unfolded the map of Canada and revealed the staggering wealth of its resources. All these things have provided the foundation, the background for Canada's markets. They, indeed, have called the markets into being. And now, we come to that practical and all-important phase which is purely and simply a consideration of the ways and means to capitalize on all these things for the development of greater business opportunity and prosperity in Canada.

All I presume to do, therefore, is to draw upon my experience, and thus suggest how any business may operate most effectively in Canada with regard to the circumstances which exist.

The topic, marketing, naturally falls into two subdivisions. These are: the nature and size of the market itself; and the functions of marketing as it applies to several geographic regions, always having regard to economic, social and political harmony.

What, then, is the market? The answer can only be—people, the customers who buy our goods and services.

Canada's people number just over fourteen and a half million— not a large population compared with most nations of the world, perhaps, but a population, nevertheless, that is growing rapidly and vigorously, decade by decade. Since 1941, Canada's population including selective immigration, has increased 22 per cent, while comparatively that of the United States has increased by 15 per cent. According to conservative estimates, we can safely forecast a population of sixteen and a half millions by 1960, and of twenty millions by 1970.

However, a population is of little value as a market unless it has

155

money to spend, so what of Canada's ability to buy? The national income, or the potential spending money, reached eighteen and a third billion in 1952—an increase of 179 per cent over 1941. Today, after taxes and dollar adjustment, the average Canadian has two-thirds more to spend or save than he had in 1938. In consequence, living standards in Canada, second only to those of the United States, have increased more than 50 per cent since 1941. Although the Canadian *per capita* income of $1,230 is still considerably below the American $1,785, the difference is steadily diminishing. By way of illustration, Canadian ownership of passenger cars has now reached the proportion of one car to every 6.7 persons, compared with the ratio of one car per 4.1 persons in the United States. This ownership has been achieved despite a tax ruling which continues to classify a motor car as a luxury. In other words, whereas the tax on a low-priced car in the United States is $134, that on a comparable model in Canada is $362!

Before leaving this fundamental topic of buying potential, it should be emphasized that the Canadian buying potential is attractive to all interests in business and industry. Canadian employment is at an all-time high, indeed, virtually 100 per cent employment prevails throughout the country. The benefits of expansion are being enjoyed in all branches of Canadian commerce and manufacturing.

Canada is in the midst of an era of unprecedented growth and spectacular development. Already, Canada is world leader in the production of nickel, newsprint, asbestos and platinum. It is the world's second largest producer of gold, aluminum, wood pulp and hydro-electric power, third in zinc, silver and uranium. Already it has become the world's third trading nation.

Turning to distribution, and to the effect of distance, climate, regional variations and other factors on the actual processes of marketing, Canada is a land of vast distances and vast area, the third biggest country in the world, yet its population of only four persons to the square mile as compared with 50.62 persons per square mile in the United States, is one of the world's sparsest. It is fortunate indeed that Canadians are a transportation-minded and a distribution-minded people. Canada developed first along the waterways of the St. Lawrence and the rivers which join it, then along the Great Lakes waterways, and finally, with a mighty surge westward, along the two transcontinental railroads. As a result, the population is concentrated in a long, narrow strip four thousand miles long and only a few hundred miles deep, within the limits prescribed by climatic conditions and rail, road and water transportation facilities. To the north lies a huge uninhabited and undeveloped area, but who can guess what hidden treasures lie buried beneath its barren surface?

It can be seen, then, that although Canada is indeed a country of vast distances, transportation, in its many forms, has simplified the problems of distribution. To move goods to market, Canada has more miles of railroad *per capita* than any other country in the world. In addition, Canada's trucking industry, which has shown tremendous growth in recent years, carries an ever larger part of the nation's goods. No fewer than 14,000 Canadian communities depend exclusively on the motor car and truck for all their transportation needs, and many of the great industrial projects currently under way in the northland would have been impossible without the assistance of motor truck transportation.

As the years go by, and more and better roads are built, and more railroads too, greater progress will be made in conquering what distribution difficulties may still remain. Already business is not as heavily concentrated in the spring and summer months as it used to be, but rather is it becoming more consistent throughout the year. A July day in Montreal or Toronto can be as sweltering as the same day in New York or Cleveland. Canadians too consume ice cream as well as pea soup, and wear tropical worsted suits and gaily coloured sports shirts when they no longer require top-coats and overshoes.

Pinpointing the market still further, we can establish the fact that large percentages of the Canadian population are highly accessible to distribution centres. The metropolitan cities of Toronto and Montreal, Winnipeg and Vancouver, each with more than a million inhabitants, together account for almost 22 per cent of our total population. Actually, there are only thirteen cities in Canada with populations in excess of 100,000, but Canada's thirty-two major urban centres represent 44 per cent of our population. The remainin 56 per cent live in smaller communities and rural areas.

Bearing in mind all these conditions, when thinking of marketing it is logical to divide Canada into five regions. These are:— the Maritime or Atlantic Provinces, Quebec, Ontario, the Prairie

Provinces and British Columbia. Distribution is organized accordingly by most Canadian companies, which maintain branches, warehouses, and sales and administrative offices which specifically serve these five separate regions.

Each region (and each of the separate provinces which make up the Maritime and Prairie regions) has its own definite temperamental, political and social characteristics which are important considerations in any business undertaking. There is a strong sense of independence on the part of each region. For example, each province has its own government, and at this moment no fewer than five political parties are in power in the ten provinces. Each region, therefore, realizing that it *is* a region, exerts its independence freely and constructively, and the prudent Canadian businessman, recognizing this fact, is always prepared to adapt and sometimes localize his merchandising, advertising and distribution policies. It is well to remember that behind the healthy spirit of competition which exists between provinces there lies a deep unity of purpose and an impregnable sense of national pride. This strong, independent regional spirit is in large part responsible for the virility and growing strength of Canada.

The most easterly of the five main regional markets is the Maritime or Atlantic group, composed of the Provinces of Nova Scotia, New Brunswick, Prince Edward Island and Newfoundland, the newest of Canada's ten provinces. It accounts for about 12 per cent of the population of Canada, and about 7 per cent of its retail business. Income is derived chiefly from the pulp and paper industry, fishing, agriculture, and, in the case of Nova Scotia only, primary iron and steel production.

Reserved and undemonstrative in many ways, the Maritimer is deeply conscious of his long establishment in North America. He is a shrewd and cautious prospect, but, once sold, he becomes a very faithful customer. He is sincere and reliable. He appreciates quiet good manners and the humour of understatement and his way of life has set the pattern for a good part of Canada, thanks to the constant emigration of Maritimers westward. There is a saying in the Maritimes that their biggest export is brains. Substantially, that is true. You will find Maritimers in many responsible positions, including the faculties of universities and colleges in Canada and the United States.

The second region is Quebec. This is Canada's oldest and largest province. It is five times the size of Texas (though vast areas of the north are uninhabited) and has a population of four millions, some 29 per cent of Canada's total.

We are witnessing at the present time one of the greatest of all feats of engineering and ingenuity, as an effort is made to obtain iron ore from the regions of Labrador. However, that project, big as it is, is making but an insignificant impression on the landscape of northern Quebec. Quebec is a province of large families. I personally have met a family consisting of twenty-six, including the parents. Anyway, it accounts for 29 per cent of the national population and about 23 per cent of the retail business. But in both respects, I can assure you that Quebec is going forward by leaps and bounds.

Here, in Quebec, superimposed upon the province's traditionally agricultural and French-speaking background, is the most startling evidence of industrial revolution, for production in that province has more than doubled in the past ten years.

This great and lovable province of Quebec has its own traditional culture and has created and sustained its own particular way of life—simple, friendly, dignified, rooted in family, church, the land and the French language. Nobody who has not experienced it can quite conceive of the gaiety, the charm, the simplicity and urbanity, which constitute the very essence of the French-Canadian temperament. They are *Canadiens* first, last and always. Among Canadians they are the first to exhibit a natural and laudable pride and affection for their homeland. Quebec is a bilingual province and that is something to bear in mind together with its other characteristics in all of your business activities and business relations.

Ontario is our third regional marketing area. This best known province—the very heart of Canada—represents one-third of the population and accomplishes half of Canada's manufacturing output. It is the largest sector of the Canadian market, nearest in approach to an industrial region by American standards.

Most Ontarians could blend quite easily into the environment of the Eastern Central States or into their cities. Ontarians tend to be staid, stable, conservative and deliberate in their way of life and in their buying habits.

They are proud of their British connections, but those connections are primarily sentimental. They enjoy doing things in the American way, because they recognize its practicality and advantages. The automotive industry is Ontario's leading industry by a wide margin, followed, not necessarily in the right order, by pulp and paper, meat packing, non-ferrous metals, primary iron and steel, rubber, machinery and agricultural implements.

Further west now, in the wide open spaces, we come to the fourth marketing region, the three Prairie Provinces of Manitoba, Saskatchewan and Alberta. The two and a half million dwellers in the Prairie Provinces, representing 18 per cent of the population, are the most approachable and the most extrovert of all Canadians. They, like their counterparts in the American Western States, tend to be hail-fellow-well-met in their personal attitudes, bold and venturesome, quick buyers and free spenders, sudden and often unpredictable in their buying patterns.

The Prairie people most clearly display the characteristics of folk who live and work and have fun in small communities. Ruggedly individualistic in their way of life, they are easily irked by any semblance of restriction or red tape. Retail business in the Prairie regions accounts for 20 per cent of the national total, and most Prairie income is derived from the land, including the petroleum underneath it.

Prairie folk are particularly susceptible to the direct, personal approach in all merchandising and sales promotional activities. They want to know all about the product they are being sold, naturally enough, but they are just as much interested in and influenced by the personality, reputation and likable qualities of the individual or organization doing the selling.

Over the Rockies, now, and into the most westerly of the five Canadian marketing regions—British Columbia, fastest-growing of all the provinces. Its population, now 8 per cent of the Canadian total, has increased a staggering $42\frac{1}{2}$ per cent since 1941, and the region accounts for some 11 per cent of the national volume of retail business.

The people of this province can point to many amazing realities to back up their high vision and optimism. Immense developments in the forest industries, the world's largest aluminum smelter, now under construction at Kitimat, British Columbia, these things are typical of the wonders taking place in this hitherto undeveloped hinterland, rich in its resources of power, mineral and forest wealth. Strongly influenced by the American West Coast, British Columbians are proud and independent. In a very special manner, the people of this region seem to be an ideal blend of British stability and American enthusiasm.

And now, what of the temperament of the Canadian people in general? We *do* have a lot of traditions that are very deeply rooted —our freely given allegiance to the Crown, for example, not because it is the *British* Crown, but because it is a symbol of unity, of loyalty, of patriotism and affection.

We are inclined to be conservative, deliberate, realistic, practical — judging things for their enduring merit rather than for their expediency. We tend to insist on quality, on stability, on goods that last longer. We pay a great deal of attention to product reputation, and our product loyalties are very strong. In the motor car business, for example, I have observed this resistance to change.

Mark you, Canadians, at the right time and in the right place— and often disastrously—are ready to place a bet at the race track or gamble on the stock markets. But, in general, we are not too responsive to "something for nothing" or to the get-rich-quick philosophy. We are rather skeptical of the so-called bargain approach, not very fond of snap judgments. We are rather reserved and proud and not too demonstrative. However, we are by no means difficult to do business with, as the record amply proves. We are not unreasonable or over-exacting, even if we do possess a kind of native caution.

As for the future of business, the outlook is most promising. Where else, in fact, is there greater scope for economic growth and business prosperity? For those who are not already established, now is the ideal time to become part of the scheme of things, to join in Canadian enterprise. For those who are now established, what could be more stimulating than the splendid prospects to which I have referred?

Despite the turmoils and repercussions of the last War, and the anxieties and frustrations of the present uneasy peace, Canadians look to the future, not just with courage, but with enthusiasm and optimism. We can and must go forward, not only to build greater prosperity and security for ourselves, but also in order to keep strong the principles of a free and honourable society.

UNIVERSITIES AND INTELLECTUAL LIFE

DR. A. W. TRUEMAN is President of the University of New Brunswick. From 1937 to 1942 Dr. Trueman was Head of the Department of English at Mount Allison University. Later he became Superintendent of Schools at St. John, New Brunswick. In 1945 he was appointed President of the University of Manitoba and remained there until 1948 when he took up his present appointment.

XVI

UNIVERSITIES AND INTELLECTUAL LIFE

IT IS THE TASK of this chapter to discuss Canada's universities and intellectual life. It shall be assumed here that Canada's intellectual life will not be too seriously neglected if discussion is confined to the first half of this double-barrelled thesis. As this chapter should be as informative as possible, the philosophy of higher education or the significance of the universities in the national life will not be considered in detail. It would be difficult to give any peculiarly Canadian cast to such statements, because inevitably they would tend to become more personal to the writer than would be proper.

What information of a helpful sort can be given about Canadian universities in one brief chapter? As a point of departure, let us choose an organization which is called the National Conference of Canadian Universities, the N.C.C.U., in this alphabetical age. All Canadian institutions of higher learning which properly may be called universities, and several which may not, are members of this organization. The name Conference which is applied to it is perhaps misleading, because the N.C.C.U. is a continuing body which holds each year a large all-Canadian Conference for its members. The rest of its activities are carried on by a permanent executive, standing and *ad hoc* committees. At the present time this Conference has thirty-two members, one of which indeed is not a university or college at all, but the National Research Council located in the capital at Ottawa. These institutions which are members of the N.C.C.U. range in size from the University of Toronto with about 11,000 students to the Nova Scotia Agricultural College, one of the earliest members of the Conference, with perhaps fewer than 200. But in addition to the thirty-two members of this national body, there are about one hundred and twenty other institutions of one sort or another which concern themselves with post-high school education: the theological colleges, and junior colleges, professional and vocational schools and in addition to these again, a considerable number of the French *collèges classiques,* for the most part located in Quebec and for the most part affiliated with the larger French universities, Laval and Montreal. Of all these two hundred or more institutions perhaps nineteen or twenty might be called universities. This figure may seem small but it must be remembered that Canada's population is only fourteen and a half million. Few people think that there are too many universities in Canada, but even if there are only nineteen or twenty to which this term may properly be applied, it is by no means certain that there are too few. It may be that Canada needs more colleges, more post-high school institutions, but that she needs more universities is an open question, if by universities is meant an aggregation of faculties representing many diverse intellectual disciplines and devoted to the task not only of maintaining and transmitting from one generation to another, the culture of the country, but also the task of enriching it and extending it.

It is an easy enough thing to set up a school. It is another matter to create and maintain a university worthy of the name. Judging only by the financial struggle in which the universities are engaged, one would be tempted to say that there is, in Canada, just about the right number. They have to fight strenuously to maintain and improve themselves and this is a most healthy state for them to be in. It is not one which university presidents are commonly supposed to enjoy, but it is a healthy state. The financial criterion, however, is not the ideal one by which to form an opinion.

Of these nineteen institutions to which the name university may be applied, six are provincial universities; nine of them are the property of, and administered by, various religious denominations both Protestant and Roman Catholic, English and French, and four of the nineteen are neither provincial nor church but private. The federal government does not maintain or control any university. It has two establishments which exist under the Department of Defence, one at Kingston, Ontario, and one at Royal Roads on the Pacific coast, but by the Canadian Constitution, the British North America Act, the provision of education facilities in the country is the responsibility and the prerogative of the various provincial governments. The charters of all these institutions are provincial in origin, not federal. The provincial governments which have provincial universities make annual grants to them ranging from the sum of $4,130,000 in the year 1952-53 for the University of Toronto in the province of Ontario down to the relatively modest sum of $350,000 per year which comes to the University of New Brunswick. But in Ontario, Quebec, New Brunswick and Nova Scotia, at least, an interesting thing takes place. The provincial governments also make annual grants in aid to non-government or non-provincial universities, that is, to church and private institutions. It is rather an interesting fact that, for instance, in Ontario, where a large sum is given to the University of Toronto, which might be described as a provincial university, considerable sums are also given to other institutions in the province, Queen's University, the University of Western Ontario and one or two more.

Perhaps this is as good a time as any to say a word or two about the part which is now being played in the financial support of Canadian universities by the federal government. For many years federal money has been directed to the universities through one channel or another. The figures for 1949-50 are revealing. In that year federal government departments and federal government agencies supplied the Canadian universities with between two and a half and three million dollars in the form of bursaries, scholarships, research fellowships, grants in aid of research and research contracts. The biggest contributors were the Department of Health and Welfare, the Defence Research Board, which is an agency of the Department of Defence, and, the biggest of all, the National Research Council, which is an agency of the Department of Trade and Commerce and located in Ottawa. In addition to that, in the same year the federal government paid out on behalf of returned soldiers registered in the universities about eighteen million dollars. This sum in Canada was spent in the form of living allowances to the veterans, in the payment of tuition fees, and in the payment of supplementary grants directly to the universities to assist them in taking care of the overhead imposed upon them by the violently increased registration and in loans to veteran students. Thus the total federal government contribution in that year on behalf of university education in one form or another was about twenty and a half million dollars. Of that sum only an estimated three million dollars can be regarded as being of direct assistance to this group of universities in helping them suport the financial burdens of the year.

In 1949 the federal government appointed a Royal Commission to make a report on the national development of the arts, letters and sciences. This report, now published, is popularly known as the Massey Report from the name of the chairman, Mr. Vincent Massey, now the Right Honourable Vincent Massey, the Governor General of Canada. The Massey Report broke new ground for the universities because it recommended in forthright form, as immediate financial assistance by the federal government to the universities, a sum of seven million dollars. This sum was completely unrestricted. It went straight into the coffers of the universities, where it rested only fleetingly before it was disbursed to reduce deficits and pacify creditors.

In the Canadian federal system, the members of the federation, that is to say, the provinces, watch the central government very closely for any signs of a disposition to encroach on provincial rights. Although every province in Canada was finding it extremely difficult to give its universities adequate financial support, every province insisted on retaining in its own hands all authority over its educational system as a constitutional right. The fears which were expressed on this point were generally quieted by the example of non-interference with provincial autonomy in the distribution of federal money on behalf of the veterans during that post-war period from 1945 until now. There are a few of the veteran students left at the universities. At any rate the federal government was able to proceed with its new scheme. It was a matter of considerable importance to the universities and roughly the scheme was as follows. With the assistance of the central university body, the N.C.C.U., the federal government drew up a list of institutions eligible for participation in the federal grants in aid. It then set aside the sum of fifty cents per head of population in each province. When the eligible institutions of each province had made a certified return of student registration to the federal government, the sum available for each province was divided among the universities of that province in exact proportion to this certified registration and was paid directly from the government in Ottawa to the universities. For example in New Brunswick the population in 1951-52 was about 530,000, in round figures. There was available for the six participating institutions in New Brunswick the total sum of about $265,000. New Brunswick that year had approximately 2,000 students in the eligible institutions. Thus the per student grant was about $132 and each institution received that amount.

One of the interesting things about this is that the provincial government did not even see the cheque. The provincial government maintained stoutly and constitutionally that it had the right, the privilege, the prerogative, to provide educational facilities. Here was a scheme whereby each university was able to receive straight from the central government a cheque as a grant in aid which did not pass through any provincial Department of Education, was not even seen by the provincial Department of Education, or by any government official. The cheque came right to the university office and all universities did exactly what their own governing body wanted to do with this money with no restrictions on it whatsoever. It was not earmarked for scholarships or for research or anything. It was just a contribution to help these institutions. Everything went as merry as a marriage bell until the province of Quebec raised the cry of provincial rights claiming that a direct payment of money to Quebec universities was a violation of the constitution and an interference with the right of the provincial government to exercise complete control over its educational system. The province of Quebec accepted the money the first year in protest and pending some clarification of the difficulty, but refused to accept it in the present year of 1952-53. That difficulty has not yet been solved. It is to be hoped that it can be and will be solved. No other province has seen fit to believe that its provincial direction of education is being endangered by the scheme as now conceived and administered. It is only fair to say that the scheme will have to be watched closely. There is always the danger that the man who pays the piper will feel that he has the right occasionally to call the tune, or at least to suggest deferentially that he would like a certain tune.

The nature of the scheme itself and its reception by Quebec and the other provinces has served to underline certain important aspects of Canadian national life, of federal existence, and of provincial rights in relation to education. That the universities of Canada need more financial assistance than they are getting is beyond dispute and one of the greatest problems is to find money for adequate salary budgets. The average salary paid in Canadian universities, to senior academics, men who are departmental heads, who have reached the status of full professors, many of whom will have served in their universities for many years, is still just below $6,000 per year and the average for associate professors is just about $5,000 per year. Since this is an average it leaps to the mind that several universities fall considerably below these averages and some of the large institutions rise considerably above them. They are few in number, but they help to bring the average up a little. Compare those figures with some from a Connecticut newspaper, which apply to the University of Connecticut. Full professors there, according to this newspaper report, enjoy a salary ranging from $6,540 to 10,140, and associate professors from $5,760 to $8,160. In each case the minimum salary is higher than the average for all Canada. No differences in the cost of living in the two countries are sufficient to offset more than slightly the difference in the salary scales. This is important. One hates to talk about money; one hates to think that one of the controlling factors in the selection of academic life as one's profession is money, but one must be realistic and this is an important fact.

What are the Canadian universities doing with the support that they have? The figures that follow must be regarded as approximate only. In what are probably the thirty leading degree conferring institutions of the country there are in this year about 58,760 students. This is a higher figure *per capita* of population than would obtain in Britain or the European countries, but lower than obtains in the United States. Last year there were about 60,380, of whom about 3,500 were veterans. For every seventeen students in attendance at Canadian universities, there is one Canadian in attendance at an American university, something like 3,800 Canadian students in the United States. It has been estimated that in slightly more than a decade in Canada the university population will double. This estimate is probably an exaggeration, but certainly the universities must prepare themselves for a large increase in enrolment, because of growing population generally and particularly because of the sharp increase in the post-war birth rate. Of this group of something like 60,000 students in the thirty leading degree conferring institutions, somewhere between fifteen and twenty thousand are registered in the Liberal Arts course. Next in order comes Engineering with about 8,300. Following the Liberal Arts and Engineering, in descending order of numbers, come Commerce and Business Administration, and the Bachelor of Science. This Spring from these institutions there will graduate about 3,550 in Liberal Arts, rather less than half that, 1,320, in Engineering, 810 in the Commerce and Business Administration courses, 750 in the Bachelor of Science, 730 in Medicine, 536 in Nursing, 350 in Household Economy or Domestic Science and 300 odd in Law.

Graduate work in Canadian universities is not yet sufficiently developed. It is a healthy and growing plant. Two universities, Toronto and McGill, one with 11,000 students and the other with something like 8,000, have each graduate schools, Toronto being slightly larger with from 750 to 800 students in the graduate school. No one would admit sooner than Toronto or McGill that these schools are not yet sufficiently supported and not yet sufficiently well-rounded. Queen's University, the University of British Columbia, and the University of Western Ontario are developing their graduate schools, but still have some distance to go before they can feel that they meet adequately their regional needs. Small graduate schools exist in say half a dozen of the other institutions.

It is very important for Canada that the development of scholarship be encouraged and broadened. The universities have done a great deal of excellent work. They have produced some distinguished men. One recalls the names of Osler and Banting in medicine, Innis and Galbraith in economics, Wrong, Webster, Martin, Brebner, Creighton, Lower and McInnis in history, Pearson in public service. The list could easily be extended. But there is much more to be done. The Canadian people generally must be brought to understand the creative force of scholarship in the life of the nation. The attitude towards scholarship is improving in Canada, there is a greater apprehension of its value to society and society's growth and enrichment. George Bernard Shaw once said, "Those who can, do; those who can't, teach", a remark which has always irked. It is a stupid remark, if one can be so daring as to apply that word to a brilliant man, because teaching is one of the noblest forms of doing, and it is a graceless remark, because Mr. Shaw, if he was ever anything in the course of his long life, was a teacher. Canadians should realize that the finest work of the universities is the indispensable, the irreplaceable contribution to the creation of the nation's culture, and the word culture is not used in its narrow sense. By it is meant vastly more than the arts which confer bloom and grace upon existence. By it is meant the whole body of thought, tradition, *mores,* and institutions, which characterizes a people, makes it what it is, contains its possibilities and hopes for the future and, as it is expressed by the Spanish writer Ortega y Gasset "saves human life from being a mere disaster. It is what enables a man to live a life which is something above meaningless tragedy or inward disgrace."

In science and technology, in trade and commerce, in the great arts, in politics and government and international relations, the scholar work of the universities is a creative force of enormous value. It cannot always provide answers to the questions of the hour. It may even appear in its various branches perversely to get off the track, but the one indispensable condition of its health and its beneficient stimulus to the growth of our civilization is that it be free. Canadians can claim that their record for the freedom of scholarship is good. They do not deny that there have been occasions when scholars have been subjected to unwise and illiberal influences, but the record has in the main been good. As far as Communism in the universities is concerned, no witch hunt has been instituted because there is very little Communism, perhaps it is fair to say almost none in the Canadian universities. Canadian universities are not perfect in this matter of freedom for scholarship, but in general the country has shown a decent regard for the principle so well stated in the words of a distinguished Canadian scholar. Mr. J. B. Brebner is a professor at Columbia University. He writes: "The societies which have succeeded best in winning and maintaining the most nearly tolerable existence for their members are those which have given free scope to their poets, artists, philosophers, scholars, inventors, adventurers, and other rebels, critics, and innovators." Canada needs especially to guard the freedom of scholars and extend hospitality to nonconformists, because she is still in the process of forming a distinct Canadian culture. It is a fair criticism to say that in the past the country and its scholars have been somewhat conservative and unadventurous in shaping the institutions and in colouring the national life. In many ways Canadians have been too derivative.

British example has meant much to Canadian universities and still does. The influence of the United States, too, has been powerful on Canada's society in general and on its universities in particular.

There is a tremendous volume of American influence, which pours into Canada like a flood from the United States, a flood of publications, radio, money.

Canadians have a profound admiration for the institutions in the United States, for the research institutes and centres, the great libraries and the great scholars without number. But they do not always feel that United States influence has been beneficial—uniformly beneficial. Therefore there is a tendency to resist it at certain points. Canada has tried, for instance, not to adopt too many American innovations in pedagogical method in secondary education, not to imitate what appears to be now and then an unabashed arithmetical computation of credits in the certification of university students for degrees, and not to include in undergraduate curricula certain irrelevant subjects which American exuberance and generosity, in some quarters at least, have taken into the academic fold.

Canada needs to pay its scholars better salaries, if for no other reason than to keep too many of them from crossing the boundary to the universities and institutes in the United States. It needs to maintain these scholars, in their freedom, increase their numbers and let them think and say and write what they want to, in order that the creative force they represent may stimulate a cautious people, give it greater self-confidence, warm it up, make its social and intellectual life more exciting and original, and fit it better for appearance on the international scene where it has begun to present a not unimpressive figure. The universities are very sound institutions, their standards are very good; the young Canadian with his B.A. or B.Sc. compares very well with any young man similarly adorned by his *alma mater*. Good foundations have been laid but these foundations must be extended. Within the limits of her resources, Canada must get on with the task of erecting on them more and richer mansions, worthy of a country which is moving steadily to a great destiny.

CANADA AND THE ARTS

Mr. Jean Chauvin is Secretary-treasurer of the Montreal magazine publishers, Poirier, Bessette and Company Limited. During World War II he served as provincial joint chairman of the Public Relations section on the National War Finance Committee. He is a Fellow of the Royal Society of Canada and a Trustee of the National Gallery at Ottawa.

XVII

CANADA AND THE ARTS

I N GIVING a brief account of Canadian art, it is perhaps best to deal chiefly with architecture and painting, their history, influences and trends, with a few words on Canadian art galleries, societies and schools. This may not seem logical, but it is, because the two most genuine expressions or manifestations of a true Canadian artistic conscience are first, the French Canadian architecture of the seventeenth, eighteenth and nineteenth centuries, and second, the painting of a certain school founded about 1920 and known as the Group of Seven. There is naturally more to be said about Canadian arts: sculpture, music, drama, ballet, ceramics, and all forms of decorative art, but all this, though interesting and worth mentioning, is not exclusively Canadian and the same may be found with local variations in any highly civilized country. To be fair, however, an exception ought to be made here of the documentary short subjects produced by the National Film Board of Canada, whose director, W. Arthur Irwin, has just been appointed Ambassador to Australia. Some of these shorts with a Canadian accent of their own, put out in the official languages of Canada, English and French, are real works of art and quite different in some respects from European or Hollywood entertainment features.

The old architecture of Quebec is the colonial architecture of France, as that of the United States is the colonial architecture of England. This is the way Ramsay Traquair summarizes it, and he adds, "The early Canadian settlers brought with them the simple building methods of the French countryside, the only methods they knew. These they adapted and modified to suit the new climate and the new living conditions of North America. So rose an architecture whose roots were French, while its blossoms were Canadian. French Canadian architecture is thoroughly French, but it is not the French of Europe. It is the French of Canada." Ramsay Traquair, an English born Canadian, an architect and author of many books, was so favourably struck by the beauty and originality of Quebec architecture that he spent his life studying and publicizing it. Many other Canadians, architects and art critics, became interested in the same subject and thanks to their researches, surveys and lectures, English speaking Canada was taken by it, so much so that the finest homes being built today in the suburbs of large cities derive from this French renaissance and Louis XIV's architecture. Most of these old houses, manors practically, rise on the banks of the St. Lawrence River between Quebec and Montreal, and on the Island of Orleans. They are rectangular buildings with low walls of white-washed stone rubble, a high roof, and a large monumental stone chimney. Craftsmen were numerous among the colonists, wood carvers and carpenters, masons and potters, coppersmiths and silversmiths, with a fine knowledge of their trade, followed later by architects, and so for a long period, two centuries at least, this architecture of French inspiration flourished in Quebec. After 1850 it lost its personal touch to become an architecture of imitation. As elsewhere in the world, architecture became conventional, banal, pretentious, and its decadence lasted until the advent of the functional architecture of today which the United States and a few European countries have given to the world.

The painters were slow to come. There were none among the early settlers. This is not surprising, for at this time Quebec and New York, or New Amsterdam, were hardly inviting places for court painters. The first painter to discover Canada was Frère Luc, or Brother Luke, a pupil of Vouet and a contemporary of Nicholas Poussin and Claude Lorrain, two French painters of the seventeenth century particularly well represented in American art galleries. Then came a few others who adhered to religious compositions and whose names nobody but historians remembers. They were followed, under the English regime at the beginning of the nineteenth century, by what we call the topographers, English army and navy officers and public servants, who were fairly good amateurs and produced some fine works and records of a documentary and sometimes artistic value. Then, around 1840, there arrived from Germany, England and France Canada's first painters of substance, Krieghoff, Jacobi, Fowler, Kane, and Berthon, who really discovered, and with a more sensitive understanding than Brother Luke, their adopted country, its wide and pleasant nature, its habitant life, the prairies, and its Indians. (We might say here that if the Indian served as a model to the painters, he never had any artistic influence on them. For the Indians—American and Canadian alike—were very far from the high degree of civilization that the Spaniards met in Mexico, Yucatan and Peru. For example, the oldest totem poles we know on the West Coast were carved with tools brought by the white man and are hardly seventy years old.) About the same time, 1850 or so, some Quebec painters appeared, who had been educated in Paris. Légaré and Plamondon among others, have left excellent portraits of the big-wigs of their time.

We come now to a fine stage of Canadian painting, influenced by the English landscapists, Turner, Constable and Bonington, by the Dutch, and, above all others, by the French impressionists and post-impressionists. We may even add to these influences that of Nordic paintings—to name one: Roerick. Some of the painters of 1900, men like James Wilson Morrice, with Tom Thomson, the most widely known Canadian painter, Clarence Gagnon, Maurice Cullen, and so forth, were clever enough to accommodate these various influences to their milieu and to work in an entirely independent manner. But the most independent, the most daring, and the first to look at Canadian scenery through Canadian eyes and in a highly decorative way of their own were the members of the Group of Seven who really struck a national note and for fifteen years, from 1915-1930, ruled over the artistic world in Canada. "Their medium," writes Graham McInnes, with Gérard Morisset, one of our best art critics, "had strength, sincerity and gusto, strong rhythmic lines and swirling patterns, clarity of atmosphere and brilliance of colour. As an art form, the work of the Group of Seven is unique and their vigour, driving power and willingness to experiment, as well as their enthusiasm, were of vital importance in the development of Canadian painting."

About this same time something similar had happened in the United States. At the turn of the century American painting, like Canadian, was trailing behind the European schools, being ignored and snubbed by the art dealers, collectors and the public at large. And this lasted until a small group of artists, known as the Eight, and later called, with mockery, the Ashcan School, brought it into the limelight. It was said lately in the *Montreal Gazette* about the recent book on the American, John Sloan, by Lloyd Goodrich, "These American artists thought that their art should be of broad prairies, rushing cities, and tall skyscrapers rather than European scenes such as mossy British trees or Paris streets transplanted in the United States. They knew that the air of this continent is lighter and the atmosphere clearer than in Europe and so they painted differently from their European contemporaries." This trend is familiar to most and the same emancipation from current influences was taking place in Mexico about the same time as the Group of Seven, 1920 or so, when Diego Rivera, Orozco and Siqueiros broke with the schools of Paris and covered the public buildings of their country, as happened in the United States at the bottom of the economic depression, with murals and frescoes, most of them as violent and one-sided as political billboards, on the tragedy of peasant life, the greedy cupidity of the rich, the struggle for workers' rights, and so forth. With them art became social and political as in Soviet Russia, with this difference, however, that Mexican painters are exceptionally good painters, that Mexican art is full of dynamism and beauty, whereas Soviet art, since the Revolution, is conservative, trivial and exceedingly dull. They say that Diego Rivera and Siqueiros are Communist. This may be, but they are Communists living and working in a free country where an artist can express himself as he pleases. Art fortunately never had any political significance in Canada. The only possible political implication that one can perceive in the whole history of Canadian art might be the emancipation from European artistic colonialism brought about by the manifesto of the Group of Seven. This pictorial movement coincided with the political maturity of the nation, conscious at last of her importance in a world that she had helped to save in the first World War by contributing nearly one million men under arms out of a population of eight million of whom 60,000 fell in the field of Flanders. The young folk of today, whose gods are named abstraction, geometry, Picasso, Braque and Mondrian, do not think much of the Group of Seven. They do not seem to realize that in spite of their undisputed talent these men are much more imitators than inventors, being the exponents of a pictorial style that we call universal, and it is universal. Although the fad for abstract painting seems to be fading away in France, where artists are switching more and more from abstractions and non-objectivism to figurative painting, it is still the fashion in most countries. The painters of abstractions and semi-abstractions may be the most vocal, but they are not the only interesting ones and those who strive to observe contemporary painting without prejudice can name at least twenty Canadian painters who still cling to a figurative art and who are, in spite of that, first rate painters and much more personal than the followers of Picasso and other *avant-garde* celebrities. There is no official art in Canada and every school of painting and sculpture from left or right wing is represented in our public collections.

This brings us to our Canadian art galleries, art societies and schools. The art gallery of today is no mere repository for the treasures of dead civilizations and a National Art Gallery, like that of Canada, located in Ottawa, the national capital, functions not for the sake of a small minority, but for the whole people. The country is enormous and the population small and scattered over ten provinces from the Atlantic to the Pacific, from the Arctic Circle to the United States boundary. The promotion of art then could not be left to private enterprise and the federal government had to intervene; hence the foundation in 1880 of the National Gallery of Canada. This institution, placed under the management of a Board of Trustees, has developed rapidly by means of annual grants by Parliament. The first Gallery, seventy years ago, was set up in a converted stable with a stock of ten paintings. Some years afterwards it received its first annual grant, a mere pittance of $5,000. Then things started to roll. A full-time Director was appointed in 1910 and also an assistant, H. O. McCurry, who took over as Director in 1939. Both of them did a grand job, squeezing money from the Treasury, buying good paintings, and helping to develop truly Canadian art. In fact they did so well that today the National Gallery of Canada receives substantial grants from the government, and its art-lending programme, its extension and education services have no parallel anywhere in the world. The National Gallery of Canada has achieved a unique position among museums and galleries for the extensiveness of its programmes and these account for about 200 separate showings each year in various parts of the country. The most important type of loan exhibition is that which is brought in from other countries for showing in Canada. Some twenty countries have been thus represented and Canadians have thereby been kept in close touch with developments abroad. Other extension methods operating within Canada include the publication of coloured reproductions, many thousands of which have been distributed to the general public, to defence establishments and to school children in connection with annual school broadcasts on the lives of Canadian artists. The National Gallery takes an active part in the promotion of films dealing with Canadian artists and in the publication of a magazine called *Canadian Art*. It has brought lecturers from abroad to tour the country. It also maintains a lending library of colour reproductions of the great masters, of films, film strips and lantern slides and of prepared lectures on art. The most recent major addition to the National Gallery's programme is the promotion of industrial design. The new Design Centre in Ottawa, under the auspices of the National Gallery, circulates exhibitions of good design and disseminates information on the subject throughout the country. The purposes of this activity are to bring the design of Canadian goods up to the best international standards.

The year 1880, which marked the official recognition of a world of arts and letters in Canada, also saw established the Royal Society of Canada and the Royal Canadian Academy of Arts, societies fashioned after the Royal Academy of England and the world famous Institut de France. Of a total membership of forty, the constitution of the Royal Academy of Arts provides for twenty-two painters, five sculptors, nine architects, four designers, etchers or engravers. Twenty-five other art societies of lesser importance exist now in Canada from the Pacific Coast to Newfoundland. As for the art schools, there are twenty-five, of which four are in Ontario, eight in Quebec, five in the Maritime Provinces, and eight in the western part of the country. To complete the statistics with art galleries and museums, these number about thirty outside the National Gallery in Ottawa, the most important being, from west to east, Vancouver, Winnipeg, Toronto, Montreal and Quebec. This all shows as briefly as possible that Canadian Art has come of age.

CANADA'S POLITICAL PHILOSOPHY

MR. GRATTON O'LEARY is Vice-president and associate editor of the *Ottawa Journal*. He spent twenty-five years in the Parliamentary Press Gallery at Ottawa, is a contributor to British, American and Canadian periodicals, and has covered international conferences over a period of thirty years.

XVIII

CANADA'S POLITICAL PHILOSOPHY

FOR MANY YEARS PAST, and notably during the last thirty years, external opinion on Canada has been preoccupied, and often confused, by political and constitutional change. This, perhaps, has been inevitable, though many Canadians have thought the preoccupation excessive and its consequences sometimes bad. That it has led to misconceptions, some amusing, not a few nonsensical, and many positively mischievous, there can hardly be a doubt. Canada has been pictured as a country which on the one hand contradicted American manifest destiny and on the other thwarted British imperialism, and whose principal role now is in one day explaining to Americans why Englishmen behave as Englishmen, and the next day explaining to Englishmen why Americans behave as Americans. This role, if it really existed, should not be belittled. Certainly it would be no mean achievement to get Brooklyn or Peoria to comprehend why Englishmen really play cricket; and one may wonder how many letters one would have to write to the London *Times* before getting the Carleton Club to grasp what a baseball immortal meant when he said that "nice guys finish last." But this role given to Canada is, of course, a fairy tale. The Canada of learned constitutions, of timid politicians, of too solemn professors and too sensational journalists has never been and is not today the Canada of the vast majority of Canadians. If excuse there be for misrepresentation, it can be found in the fact that a country which is American geographically, British politically, and largely French in origin almost inescapably affords subject matter for the exercise of imagination.

What actually is Canada's political philosophy? Lord Oxford once said that history is philosophy teaching by examples. This is the pattern, this is the clue which must be followed by anyone seeking to discover or define a political philosophy for Canada. As a point of departure it may be said that Canada's philosophy or group psychology is still in process of expression in the pragmatic way, that Canadians want to be the architects of their history and not its slaves, and that they will refuse to yield to any deterministic cynicism that would be unworthy of their democratic faith.

Canada was established as a self-governing dominion with national aspirations in 1867, about three-quarters of a century after the coming of the Constitution of the United States. There were then in Canada some three million people assuming responsibility for the future growth and development of half a continent, the western part of which was practically unpopulated, undeveloped, and politically and socially unorganized. No Declaration of Independence, no Bill of Rights marked the year of Confederation. The "Kingdom" of Canada was suggested as a name by the chief founder and first Prime Minister, John A. Macdonald, but in one of the earliest gestures of the good neighbour policy it was dropped, out of regard to the United States, and changed to "Dominion". Today, after eighty-five years of tests and experiments, of hard campaigns with some lost battles, Canada's democratic loyalties have crystallized and deepened. Canada was not founded on republicanism but on the doctrine of constitutional liberty under the symbol of the British Crown. Her political philosophy had its roots in the traditions and the common law of England. Macaulay, in a flight of imagination, once pictured an Australian lying out under the Southern Cross and reading by its light those unforgettable words from Magna Carta: "To no man shall we sell, to no man delay, to no man deny justice and right." An equally picturesque pen could have written similarly of Canada. The substance of the Canadian system is the regard for human freedom. Canada's philosophy, therefore, in so far as example has been able to reveal it, seems to be forming rapidly into a conscious national unity and pride, but with this pride and unity joined to respect and regard for the peoples of other nations. Her international outlook is essentially North American and Western Hemisphere but over all, and throughout the world, Canadians believe that they should respect those things which they may not yet understand, that in the words of the noble American jurist, Learned Hand, they should not try to scourge from the temple those who do not see with their eyes.

Some one may ask, How can Canada claim to be North American and Western Hemisphere and yet give allegiance to a Queen? The reply must be that devotion to freedom, that exercise of democracy in the highest degree can exist outside the fold of republicanism, that it does, in fact, exist under the Crown in Canada and throughout the British Commonwealth. Most Canadians have little patience with nonsensical talk about the "magic" of monarchy. They do subscribe, though, to what was said only recently by their Governor General, representative of Elizabeth II, who is not only England's Queen but also Queen of Canada. This is what he said: "We in Canada do not forget that the institutions of Crown and Parliament embodying the ideals of liberty and authority are on this continent peculiarly ours. It is we who have cherished and preserved them in the New World. It is we who can offer them, in our own Canadian translation, as our contribution to civilized life on this continent. The combination of this symbol of authority with humanity is a not unworthy contribution which Canada makes to North American life."

The average Canadian does not easily define in words the loyalties that bind him to those institutions of Crown and power but he does know instinctively, what such a system means to him. It means to him democracy with graciousness and good manners. It means his right to go about the daily business of living as a free man equal before the law to those who sit in the seats of the mighty. It means the right to think what he pleases, and to say openly what he thinks, and to vote as his own judgment bids him vote. It means the right to worship in his own way according to his own conscience. It means the right to live under a system of government deriving its just powers from the consent of the governed. It means a parliament where opposing views are represented, where ideas are not merely uttered but debated, and where men who are free to speak are also compelled to answer. It means the right to be secure against arbitrary power of whatever kind, against the bad politician who would suppress free speech no less than against the drumhead court and the dry rot of the concentration camp. It means the right to follow according to his own lights and without dictation from any ruling clique of the state the pursuit of liberty as he has known it and of happiness as he has hoped to find it. About these things there need be no doubt whatever. They are of the very heart, the very essence of the Canadian spirit, just as they are of the heart and essence of the spirit of America.

And what, it may be asked, of the French speaking Canadians? In Canada today there is no racial problem, no racial disunity. A French Roman Catholic is the Prime Minister of Canada. A French Canadian Roman Catholic is the Chief Justice of the Supreme Court. French Canadians sit in the House of Commons, in the Senate, in the provincial legislatures and all of the governing authorities. In a country with a majority of English and Protestants these facts hardly tell of disunity and certainly do not tell of intolerance or bigotry. The truth is that French and British Canadians have a growing fund of common fears and hopes and experiences and to that extent can be regarded as one people. Only one thing should be added: while Canada is the inheritor of the traditions of the two great races of Britain and France, there is nevertheless a Canadian mosaic of peoples. It is not one tributary, but the co-operation of all that has fed the waters and guided the currents of the main stream. Canada, like the United States, has had its melting pot and mostly she has found it good.

This sense of union is revealed most of all in Canada's external relations. Any Canadian government, like any American government, must have its foreign policy shaped by the necessity of preserving national unity as far as possible and by taking no action lightly which might disturb violently the relations of one part of the country with another. Sharply revealing, therefore, is the fact that Canada's membership in the United Nations, her signature to the Atlantic Treaty, and her decision to spend vastly more on defence, have brought nothing but support from all classes of her people. Liberals and Conservatives may disagree deeply in domestic policies. Quebec's outlook in some things is different from Ontario's, but in foreign affairs, in the determination to defend their democratic way of life, Canadians stand absolutely as one. There are signs even of the sun going down on the old wrath of military conscription. This from past years is a considerable gain.

Canadians are apt to chide Americans for their isolationism in the 1920's and 1930's, to recall reproachfully the fate of Woodrow Wilson over the League of Nations, yet in those same 1920's and 1930's Canada too had her isolationists, a period when from the banks of the Ottawa River the light of Geneva seemed dim, and when a Canadian government had nailed to its mast-head the watchword, "No commitments." Today with the atom bomb and Moscow's spectre that isolationism is dead. No Canadian government now and no Canadian party could preach isolationism and live. There is something here that in all conscience should be added. Some Canadians today speak vaingloriously of Canada as a middle power. Some of them go about with a nationalist chip on their shoulder, but the sane majority are without delusions of grandeur, understanding well that Canada must have something to offer the world beyond vanity and suave internationalism, that a passion for distant freedom is not enough and that she cannot expect to export democracy unless and until it is produced at home. Much has been said in this book of the discoveries of vast new wealth, of unimaginable riches under the soil of Canada. For these gifts of fortune Canadians are grateful. Yet they are trying to remember the warning which James Russell Lowell once spoke to his fellowcountrymen, the warning that the true greatness of a nation must be weighed in scales more delicate than the balance of trade.

Much has been written in the United States and Canada about the Report by a Canadian body with the rather frightening name of a Royal Commission on the National Development of the Arts, Letters and Sciences. This report followed an enquiry described by an American educationalist as a search for a Canadian accent. In fact, not too many Canadians were impressed with the idea of this Royal Commission or with the character of much of its report, this for the simple reason of their belief that culture cannot be purchased, cannot be planned, and cannot be conscious, and for the further reason that there is no sense in pasting wings on man unless you can give him a winged nature. If a nation gives to its people true education, culture will take care of itself. "Culture," writes T. S. Eliot, "can never be wholly conscious. It cannot be planned because it is also the unconscious background of our planning. We cannot directly set about to create or improve culture. We can only will the means which are favourable. One thing to avoid is a universalized planning. One thing to ascertain is the limits of planning."

With this digression, this chapter ends where it began with the contention that the people of Canada, like the people of the United States, are North Americans, inheritors of the thought and traditions of Europe, but also the children of geography, products of the emotions, the driving forces, the faith, the dreams, and the forms of expression of the North American continent. Many foolish things have been spoken and much solemn nonsense written about the relations between these two peoples. Indeed there are still foolish people, still demagogues and ultra-nationalists who write evil things about the two countries. It is said that for a century Canadians and Americans have had peace by friction. It is argued that for a hundred years Canadians lived in the shadow of the fear of annexation, and it is being said now, said by shallow, mischievous so-called pundits, that Canadians are in terror of "American Imperialism." Much has been made, much fiction written, about the War of 1812. The truth, of course, is that no one has ever quite discovered what it was all about, even though, as one wit put it, it made awfully great pictures. It ended, of course, in a draw, though not according to respective school books of the two countries, and the governments, sorry and ashamed, made peace without a single reference being made to the supposed causes of the conflict. There was, too, the Civil War in the United States. That war may have hastened Confederation in Canada but no one can ever say that Canadians were against Americans then, seeing that, as a matter of fact, and as the great Canadian humorist Stephen Leacock was quick to point out, Canada sprang to the help of both sides. Canadians fought in the Northern armies and lent money to the South, and when everything was over exulted with the North, shed a tear with the South, and have been glorifying Lincoln and the Union ever since.

In Canada's capital, the city of Ottawa, there is an old canal which winds through the town. Weeping willows grow beside it and arch over it and not one Canadian in ten thousand knows when or why it was built. It was built more than a century ago by a British engineer to help defend Canada against the United States; and the fact that today this old canal is but a museum piece, its origin unknown or unremembered, tells the blessed thing that has come between these two countries and which today has roots deeper than before. The United States has reached to a primacy of power with an awesome accountability to history. In that decisive role, in all that it must call for in wisdom and patient courage, Canadians will be true allies, good neighbours, staunch friends. When Canada has taken her share in beating down evil, she will be willing to take the same share in setting up good, knowing that her day is tomorrow. This, is Canada's philosophy and faith.

CANADA-UNITED STATES RELATIONS

THE HONOURABLE H. HUME WRONG is the Ambassador of Canada to the United States. In 1927 he was appointed First Secretary to the Canadian Legation in Washington and later Counsellor. From 1937 to 1939 he was a permanent delegate to the League of Nations. Shortly after the outbreak of war he was sent to London as a special economic adviser. He later returned to the Canadian Legation in Washington. In 1942 he was appointed Assistant and then Associate Under-Secretary of State for External Affairs. He became Ambassador in 1946.

XIX

CANADA-UNITED STATES RELATIONS

IN THIS BOOK on Canada, a great deal has already been said inevitably about the relations between Canada and the United States. This chapter will discuss these relations in the difficult context of Canada's future. The writer is not equipped with the mantle of a prophet; he has no crystal ball nor a convenient oracle to enable him to peer into the future. There is, then, no intention here to attempt the impossible by trying to predict what the relationships between Canada and the United States will be in the years to come. It may, however, serve to cast some light on what the future may bring if, as a point of departure, a description is given of two extreme views, both now current, of the position of Canada in relation to the United States. Later, some thoughts on the realities will be offered.

First let us consider how the relations between Canada and the United States appear to Communist eyes behind the Iron Curtain. According to Communist theory and practice, to judge from what is publicly said and written, and very probably widely believed, Canada can only be a satellite or a victim for the United States, and probably both. The bloodthirsty exploiters of Wall Street, they may say, have stretched their greedy hands across the international boundary in order to exact tribute from the Canadian people who are powerless to resist. The monopolists of American industry and finance, aided by their traitorous Canadian minions, are constantly frustrating developments in Canada which are strongly desired by Canadians in their own national interest. They might conclude that Canadians have nothing to lose but their chains, and that the way to cast off these chains is to transform Canada into what they call a people's democracy.

To the devout Communist peering in the direction of North America through the Iron Curtain, how must the relationships between Canada and the United States appear? He sees two very

large countries dividing between them all but the southern
extremities of the North American continent. He notes that the
boundary between them is of phenomenal length, the longest
boundary possibly between any two countries in the world, and
that this boundary splits in half four of the five Great Lakes,
follows the course of the St. Lawrence, Detroit and other rivers, and
for a great stretch of its total length is an arbitrary line marked by no
natural features. He concludes, rightly, that the affairs of two
countries linked so extensively by geography, must be very much
mixed up. He observes that one of the countries is the wealthiest
and most productive country in the world, while the other has only
about one-eleventh of its population and perhaps one-fifteenth of
its production; furthermore, that the resources of the weaker country
are very great and in the process of rapid development, a development much aided by the willingness of the capitalists of the United
States to invest large sums in Canada. He learns that a substantial
portion of Canadian industry is owned or controlled by large concerns in the United States, and he notes the enormous volume of
trade that crosses the international boundary and the huge flow of
persons constantly going from one country to the other.

Now, all these observations are perfectly true. The list of facts
which establish the intimacy of the relations between the two
countries could be extended almost *ad infinitum.* Where our faithful Communist would go wrong is in the deductions which he is
compelled by his rigid doctrine to draw from the facts. For he is
compelled to conclude, or to assert that he concludes lest he be
found guilty of the horrid crime of deviation—a crime which may
now be in process of redefinition—that Canada is a prime example
of the economic imperialism with which he charges the United
States. He is compelled to believe therefore that Canadian political
independence is only maintained because Canada is an obedient
satellite, as ready to obey the master's voice as are the unfortunate
Soviet satellites in Europe, and that Canadian independence is
nominal, not real, preserved only for the convenience of the
American exploiters.

Such Communists would only be confirmed in their mistaken
views if they pondered the probable course of future developments.
To select two illustrations: try to imagine how they would look
at the needs of the United States for raw materials and at the

problems of North American defence. They could truthfully note that the need for raw materials to satisfy the huge demand of American industry is steadily increasing, that a growing proportion of these materials must be secured from other countries, and that great new resources are under development in Canada for which the United States will be a principal market. From this must they not deduce, following their mistaken dogma, that Canada must become more and more the servant of the monopolists of the United States?

Turning to defence, the Communists might argue that as the range and destructive power of new weapons increase and as the value of the protection afforded by oceans and icy wastes diminishes, Canada is in process of becoming the front line of defence against attack on the United States from the north, the bastion which protects the heartland of American industry. Surely, then, would they not say, Canada must be under the military direction and control of the United States, for reasons similar to those which have led the Soviet Union to surround itself with a defensive ring of satellites in Europe. Such an interpretation comes naturally to the Communist mind, obsessed with the idea of inevitable conflict.

Let us turn from this extreme view to another but opposite extreme attitude which is closer to the truth but nevertheless requires considerable modification. This view is sometimes expressed in passages of flamboyant oratory, more frequently perhaps in the United States than in Canada. It depicts the cordial relations which exist between the two countries as part of the natural order of things, with the two governments and the two nations bound together indissolubly in brotherly love. Even admitting that this condition has not always existed in the past, these extremists would maintain that a state of opinion and a degree of interdependence have now been developed which guarantee its continuance in perpetuity. So many pleasant and complimentary things are currently being said about Canada in the United States that if one had a really sinister mind one might suspect a concerted American design to infect the Canadian people with a bad case of what the Greeks called *hubris*, a vainglorious pride which would only be a prelude to their destruction. That, of course, is bunkum; but it is both nice and novel to have so much attention paid to Canadian accomplishments and Canadian prospects.

On the one hand we must emphatically reject the Communist interpretation that, no matter what we say, Canada is a victim, willing or unwilling, of American exploitation. On the other hand the opposite error must not be made of assuming that everything will always go well without anyone ever having to do anything very much about it.

The truth is that Canadians and Americans get on well together not because of any superior or inherent national virtue. This state of affairs has not come into existence without a lot of effort, nor will it continue automatically. The two nations do indeed have a great deal in common in their standards of behaviour, their conception of justice, as well as in their national interests. They share a continent which in the dislocated and frenzied world of today is one of the safest places in which to live and also the richest and most comfortable to be found anywhere.

Canada and the United States have indeed reached a position in which their peoples can proudly say that their relationship is a fine example to the rest of the world. That has not always been the case. It has not come about from natural circumstances unassisted by human endeavour. It is the product of many years of development, through many ups and downs, guided by some wise statesmanship and buttressed by tolerant recognition of national interests, national feelings, and, indeed, national prejudices on both sides of the international boundary. The qualities of restraint, imagination and understanding which have helped to produce the present welcome results are still needed just as much as ever to preserve them. These qualities may indeed be needed more than ever today because of the rapidity in this era of technical achievement of the process of shrinkage of space and time.

As mankind progressively masters space and time, so does the area of international relationships automatically expand, and so consequently do the possible sources of international friction increase. For most of the last quarter of a century the present writer has been involved in one capacity or another with a share of the conduct of official business between the governments of the United States and Canada. He has seen that business enlarge greatly, indeed enormously, in extent. Many subjects now of the highest importance and urgency in the official relations of the two countries never entered into them at all twenty-five years ago. Just as there is need to achieve a meeting of minds between Washington and Ottawa on many grave matters which each government once regarded as outside the realm of its international affairs, so new and prickly problems of mutual concern arise which are deeply involved in the domestic politics of both countries.

There still remain the old issues with which the peoples of Canada and the United States have lived for many years. To give a few examples: there are still ancient differences about trade and tariffs, intricate difficulties over customs regulations, though that is predominantly a one-sided issue with the complaints mainly of Canadian origin, still the inability up to the present to arrive at final agreement on how to make joint use of the water power which runs to waste in the international section of the St. Lawrence River and, therefore, the inability to link the inland seas of the Great Lakes with the Atlantic Ocean by an adequate channel of navigation. Such issues as these are old friends, or enemies, perhaps nearer resolution, but as important today as they ever were. They have not been superseded, but they have been supplemented by many newer issues. The outcome is that never have the official relations between Canada and the United States been so close and friendly as they are now, but also never have they been so complicated and so difficult. More than goodwill is required to avoid future irritations, recriminations and disputes. More than ever are needed the stern virtues of sober judgment, hard work, and recognition of the general interest over local pressures and demands.

Of course, the relationships between the two countries involve much more than the dealings between the two governments. They comprise the countless contacts for pleasure and for profit, for friendship and for business, between Americans and Canadians. A continuous effort, both private and public, is needed to bring about a better understanding in both countries of each other's interests, problems and potentialities. The two democracies, while equally based on the will of the people, must reach their governmental decisions independently and by different constitutional methods. It is of high importance to all that they should find their way together in amity and constancy of purpose through the mazes, the entanglements, the frustrations and the perils of today.

CANADA'S ECONOMIC FUTURE

THE RIGHT HONOURABLE C. D. HOWE, following a distinguished career in the field of engineering, was elected to the House of Commons in 1935. After holding many important posts in the Government of Canada, he was appointed Minister of Trade and Commerce in 1948. With the establishment of a Department of Defence Production in 1951, Mr. Howe was appointed Minister of Defence Production, while retaining his portfolio as Minister of Trade and Commerce. Mr. Howe has been a member of the Imperial Privy Council since 1946.

XX

CANADA'S ECONOMIC FUTURE

THE CHAPTERS WHICH have preceded this were contributed by an outstanding group of spokesmen for Canada, each of them eminent in his field. They have conveyed a clear and balanced picture of almost every aspect of the Canadian people, their industry, and their culture, their international problems and their domestic problems, their past and their future. It is difficult enough to add more to this wealth of information from others and the difficulties are increased by the subject which has been allotted for discussion in this chapter. It is the one subject on which there is no available information whatsoever, namely the future. True enough, the subject has been narrowed down to the economic future as distinct from the whole future, but even with regard to the economic future no special gift of clairvoyance is claimed by this writer. In looking to the future, then, there is no intention here of making factual economic predictions. These may be left to others with more vigorous imaginations. Some present trends, however, have obvious implications for the future and these can clearly be seen, even if in somewhat general terms.

References are often made to what is called the "Canadian boom". If this phrase implies that Canada is expanding and prosperous, the description is accurate enough. Sometimes, however, the word "boom" suggests a temporary and artificial prosperity accompanied by inflation and excessive speculation, and ending inevitably in a bust. In that sense there is no Canadian boom and anyone who goes to Canada looking for one will be disappointed. Indeed, what must strike most observers as remarkable is the almost complete absence of boom psychology in Canada. There was a good deal more excitement and speculation in the years prior to World War I when the wheat areas of the prairie west were being brought under the plough, and of course during the late 1920's. Yet at present the country is expanding about as rapidly as during any period in its history and on a much broader front. Even before the outbreak of war in Korea, and the accompanying increase in defence preparations, capital expenditures in Canada were running at high levels and rising. Unemployment was at a minimum. The country was just at the beginning of the new industrial era. Korea necessitated some change of direction to give more priority to the production of essential materials but it made little difference to the overall rate of expansion. The economy was already working close to capacity and showed every sign of continuing to do so. Canada had no hesitation in rallying to the defence of the free world when necessity arose. Let no one think, however, that there is any profit in it for Canada. Canadians would prefer to be devoting their resources and energies entirely to raising the standards of living of their own people and those in other lands. Those who look upon this as an ordinary boom, then, or attribute Canadian prosperity and expansion to world rearmament, miss the true significance of what is happening in this country. Shakespeare said that "there is a tide in the affairs of men which, taken at the flood, leads on to fortune". Perhaps this is true also of nations, for one can usually mark a period in its history when each of the leading nations of the modern world seems to gather strength and suddenly take great strides forward in wealth and power. It is not improbable that Canada is passing through such a period. It is as if each discovery and development leads to others in a chain reaction.

The turning point in Canada came with the discovery, after many years of disappointment, of a major oil field on the prairies. This discovery coincided closely with the uncovering of vast reserves of iron ore in Quebec-Labrador. Thus almost over night Canada made good her two most serious deficiencies as an industrial power, oil and iron. The development of these resources required the building of pipelines and railways and the provision of power. Quebec-Labrador iron provided the final and convincing reason why the building of the St. Lawrence Seaway is necessary without further delay to provide transportation for Canada's expanding commerce. The conclusion is inescapable, therefore, that this is not an ordinary boom dependent upon rearmament or otherwise. Behind it lies something much more fundamental which will persist for years to come, carried along by its own inner momentum.

It has also been suggested that Canadian prosperity and expansion are to a large extent dependent upon the defence preparations of the free world, and that if, as the saying goes, peace breaks out, the structure would collapse. Any sudden reduction in defence expenditures, particularly in the United States, would, of course, have a profound effect upon the course of business not only in Canada but throughout the world, but Canada would be no more sensitive to such a development than any other country and probably less sensitive than most. Too much attention, however, should not be concentrated on what happens if economic prospects deteriorate. The fear of depression has obscured clear thinking about many economic problems and has led on some occasions to serious errors of judgment in public policy in many countries.

The second major point in looking to the future is related to the first and yet distinct. It has to do with the abundance of Canadian natural resources, which promise to give Canada an increasingly important place in world industry and trade. In Canadian-American relations this means that the United States is becoming more important to Canada as a market. Reference has been made in this connection to iron ore, copper, lead, zinc, timber and petroleum, for all of which the United States must look forward to dependence upon imports from the outside world. Similar conditions of scarcity now exist in many parts of the world. Canada is at this same time in possession of vast and increasing resources of many of these very materials of which other countries are short. Much has been written about potential Canadian wealth in iron, oil, nickel, uranium, silver, titanium, and a wide range of other minerals. She has impressive forest reserves and on her wide prairies produces the world's fourth largest crop of wheat. Canada is the leading supplier of newsprint, nickel, and asbestos. Her reserves of base metals, coal, iron and oil have stirred the imaginations of people everywhere. This great storehouse promises much to the future of the world as well as to the economic future of Canada. The promise might be less if these resources were being dissipated wantonly and without regard for the future, but this is not the case. In her timber and pulp and paper industries there is widespread and growing interest in the conservation of reserves and in complete utilization of felled timber. In agriculture increasing attention is being given to the best uses of land. In petroleum and natural gas development the most modern techniques of exploration and of efficient exploitation are already in use in an industry which is still in its infancy. These great natural assets are not being thrown away or wasted. They are indeed still being increased. It is fortunate that the commodities Canada is best able to produce are ones of which the world stands in greatest need.

The third point is that the problems to be seen ahead for Canada have mostly to do with the external situation, with world trade and with international finance. They are really world economic problems in which Canada is involved rather than specifically Canadian problems. Canadians have, in fact, very few worries about the internal structure of the Canadian economy. It is in good balance. Its rate of growth in recent years has been prodigious. The productivity of the Canadian people is high. The government is strong and its policies sound.

These are the three major points about the Canadian economic future: that Canada's development is well founded, that her resources are great and growing, and that she looks hopefully to co-operation with other countries to solve the problems that she can see ahead.

Before concluding this discussion of Canada's internal economy, a word should be said on a subject that Canadians regard as most urgent, namely the further improvement of the St. Lawrence Seaway. The apparent unwillingness of the government of the United States to extend the small degree of co-operation required to enable Canada to proceed with this project puzzles Canadians completely. Perhaps a few words will explain the Canadian viewpoint. The seaway from Lake Erie to the Atlantic Ocean lies wholly within Canada except for some 115 miles where the river forms a boundary between the province of Ontario and the state of New York. Within this common boundary there is a stretch of forty-seven miles of river known as the international rapids section which provides a major obstacle to navigation. Since some form of joint action between Canada and the United States is required for the economical development of this forty-seven miles of river, Canada's desire to improve further its outlets to the ocean can be, has been, and is being, frustrated by lack of co-operative action by the United States Congress. The importance of the St. Lawrence Seaway to the Canadian economy has been recognized by Canadians throughout the last century. The grain crops of the western prairies move to market by that route, just as raw and finished materials from the lower St. Lawrence and from abroad move into central and western Canada in the other direction.

The first improvements of the seaway date back a full century. The first canal system provided for nine-foot navigation. This was followed by canals and locks allowing fourteen-foot draught. Later the waterway above the international section was improved for twenty-seven foot draught by the construction of the new Welland Canal below Lake Erie. The river below Montreal has been improved to provide a channel to the ocean having a minimum width of six hundred feet and a depth of thirty-five feet. The bottleneck in the Seaway, fourteen-foot navigation in the international rapids section, would have been removed by Canada long since had the government of the United States extended the necessary co-operation. It should be noted at this point that the St. Lawrence Seaway is, and always has been, a Canadian seaway. Every important improvement has been built and paid for by Canada from Lake Erie down. The cost of operating and maintaining the Seaway is paid wholly by Canada. Nevertheless, ships of every nation may use the Seaway without payment of tolls. An international treaty provides that if and when tolls on shipping are imposed they will bear equally on Canadian and foreign flag ships. Canada proposes to pay, on a self-liquidating basis, for improvement in the international rapids section. Why, then, should the United States withhold its co-operation and thus delay completion of this vital Canadian transportation outlet? The drop of the river in the international rapids section makes possible the development of a large block of low-cost hydro-electric power to be shared equally by the two countries. Economy dictates that this hydro power be developed either prior to or as part of the Seaway development. Canada is ready and anxious to develop its share. It is known that the state of New York would like to develop the share of the United States. But necessary federal permission has not been granted either to New York state or to some other competent agency. Canada can and will proceed to remove the bottleneck in her twenty-seven foot navigation channel from Lake Erie to the ocean, as soon as competent authorities are authorized to build the power development.

Proposals are now being advanced that the United States should build a new canal in the international rapids section. Such a proposal can only complicate the present situation. Ownership by the United States of a short section of a very long Seaway would only add to the overall construction costs and would complicate problems of maintenance and operation of the canal system. It seems obvious that continued ownership by one national authority of the entire Seaway represents the most efficient procedure. There are critical channels between the upper Great Lakes which will require deepening to twenty-seven feet at some stage and by assuming responsibility for such deepening the United States can take on a much more logical and valuable role by making twenty-seven foot navigation possible throughout the upper Great Lakes to conform with the navigation depths to be provided in the all-Canadian St. Lawrence Seaway. Perhaps this reference to the Seaway is hardly appropriate to the subject of this book. But the subject is *Canada: Nation on the March* and Canada can hardly march if she is to be handicapped by a serious lack of internal transportation. An adequate St. Lawrence Seaway is essential to Canada's further economic progress.

It is not very practical to speculate about the economic future of Canada in any more concrete terms than those which have been outlined here. What is much more interesting about the economic future is what is being done about it today. Canadians are confronted with large-scale economic problems to be considered and dealt with. Future economic trends are in their hands now to be shaped for better or for worse. These constitute Canada's relationship to the future because she is deciding now in what direction she is going to go. If Canada can successfully resolve her present problems, the future will take care of itself.

The surest guide and the only guide to the future is in the past. Canada has demonstrated an ability to deal with day to day problems with some success. That thought leads one to view the future prospects of Canada with great confidence.

COMMITTEES IN CHARGE OF THE
TOWN HALL SERIES

FOR THE TOWN HALL, INC.

Mrs. Elinore Herrick *Chairman*

Dr. Thurston J. Davies

Dr. John H. Powell, Jr.

PLANNING COMMITTEES

IN THE UNITED STATES	IN CANADA
Mr. Lyttleton B. P. Gould *Chairman*	Mr. Don Henshaw *Chairman*
	Mr. I. S. Decarie
Mr. B. H. Holdsworth	Mr. Douglas Gibson
Mr. William Honneus	Mr. Bruce Keith
	Mr. Ivan Lenard
Mr. Taylor Mills	Mr. John Martin
Dr. John H. Powell, Jr.	Mr. Frank Prendergast

CANADIAN SPONSORING COMMITTEE

Mr. H. L. Enman *Chairman*

Mr. G. Maxwell Bell

Mr. Ralph P. Bell

Mr. George W. Bourke

Mr. Aden Bowman

The Hon. Philippe Brais

Mr. Edward E. Buckerfield

Mr. C. L. Burton

Mr. Philip A. Chester

General H. D. C. Crerar

Dr. A. H. S. Gillson

Mr. A. E. Grauer

Mr Joseph Harris

Mr. H. G. Hilton

Mr. Charles E. Hunt

Dr. F. Cyril James

Dr. A. E. Kerr

The Hon. Ray Lawson

Dr. Norman A. M. MacKenzie

Dr. W. A. Mackintosh

Mr. H. R. MacMillan

Mr. J. W. McConnell

Mr. H. Ray Milner

Mr. James Muir

Mr. J. Y. Murdock

Mr. Gratton O'Leary

Mr. Lazarus Phillips

Mr. Marshall Porter

Senator C. C. Pratt

Mr. D. B. Rogers

Mr. Herbert H. Rogge

Mr. Rhys M. Sale

Mr. Lewis W. Simms

Dr. Sidney Smith

Dr. Andrew Stewart

Mr. G. L. Stewart

Mr. E. P. Taylor

Dr. A. W. Trueman

Msgr. Ferdinand Vandry

Mr. W. A. Wecker

Mr. Stanley M. Wedd

Mr. W. Garfield Weston

UNITED STATES SPONSORING COMMITTEE

Dr. Henry T. Heald *Chairman*

Mr. I. C. R. Atkin

Mr. Kenneth C. Bell

Mr. Harold Blancke

Mr. Albert Bradley

Mr. Hugh Bullock

Mr. Harold W. Comfort

Dr. Thurston J. Davies

Mr. Morse Dial

The Hon. Lewis W. Douglas

Mr. R. K. Ferguson

Mr. Clarence Francis

Mr. Duncan W. Fraser

Mr. G. Keith Funston

Mr. William T. Gossett

Mr. Lyttleton B. P. Gould

Mr. Henry H. Hewetson

Mr. John Jay Hopkins

Mr. Edward T. McCormick

Mr. E. C. McDonald

Mr. Clarence J. Myers

Mr. Ralph T. Reed

Mr. Howard C. Sheperd

Mr. Harold M. Stewart

Mr. William C. Stolk

Mr. C. B. Thomas

Dr. John F. Thompson

Mr. George Van Gorder

INDEX

DATE DUE

Jau 2
Mar 27
ap 24
Oct 26
Feb 15

DATE DUE